Ninja Foodi Digital Air Fryer Oven

Cookbook

Super Easy 1800 Days of Tasty & Low-Carb Air Fryer Recipes for Beginners and Advanced Users | Air Roast, Air Broil, Bake, Bagel, Toast, Dehydrate and more

Thad R. Watson

CONTENTS

Vegetables And Vegetarian 65

Lunch And Dinner 75

INTRODUCTION

Thad R. Watson is a seasoned culinary expert with a flair for innovation in the kitchen. With over two decades of experience as a professional chef and a passion for exploring the latest cooking technologies, he has established himself as a leading authority in the world of modern kitchen appliances. Thad's journey into writing "The Ninja Foodi Digital Air Fryer Oven" was a natural progression of his career.

Inspired by the revolutionary capabilities of the Ninja Foodi Digital Air Fryer Oven, Thad embarked on a mission to share his expertise and discoveries with home cooks everywhere. He spent countless hours experimenting with this versatile appliance, pushing its boundaries to uncover its full potential. His goal was to demystify the art of air frying, roasting, baking, and dehydrating, making these techniques accessible to anyone seeking flavorful, healthy, and time-efficient meals.

Thad's unique blend of culinary artistry and technical insight shines through in his book, as he breaks down complex cooking processes into easy-to-follow steps. He brings a deep understanding of flavors, textures, and techniques to the table, helping readers harness the power of the Ninja Foodi Digital Air Fryer Oven to create restaurant-quality dishes in the comfort of their own homes.

In "The Ninja Foodi Digital Air Fryer Oven," Thad R. Watson shares his passion for cooking, his culinary wisdom, and his innovative recipes, inviting readers to embark on a culinary journey that promises delicious, convenient, and health-conscious dining experiences. As an accomplished chef, Thad's mission is to empower individuals to unleash their inner chef and elevate their cooking game with this remarkable kitchen appliance.

WHAT IS NINJA FOODI DIGITAL AIR FRYER OVEN?

The Ninja Foodi Digital Air Fryer Oven is a multifunctional kitchen appliance that seamlessly combines the convenience of an air fryer, the versatility of a convection oven, and the precision of a digital cooking device. With its spacious interior and a range of cooking modes, including air frying, roasting, baking, broiling, and dehydrating, this appliance enables users to prepare a wide variety of dishes with crispy, golden results while reducing oil usage and ensuring even cooking. Its user-friendly digital interface and customizable settings make it a valuable addition to any kitchen, providing an efficient and healthier way to achieve delicious meals and snacks with ease.

Cooking function

Air Fry   Roast   Bake   Broil

Dehydrate   Reheat   Keep Warm

CONVENIENCE AND HEALTH BENEFITS OF IT

Versatility: The Ninja Foodi Digital Air Fryer Oven can replace multiple kitchen appliances, such as a traditional oven, toaster oven, dehydrator, and deep fryer. This saves you counter space and reduces clutter in your kitchen.

Air Frying: Air frying is a healthier cooking method compared to deep frying. The Ninja Foodi uses convection heating and a powerful fan to circulate hot air around the food, crisping it up with little to no oil. This results in delicious, crispy meals with significantly less fat and fewer calories.

Reduced Oil Consumption: With the air frying feature, you can enjoy your favorite fried foods with up to 75% less oil than traditional frying methods. This is beneficial for those looking to cut down on their fat intake.

Healthier Cooking: The Ninja Foodi Digital Air Fryer Oven allows you to prepare healthier meals by eliminating the need for excessive oil, making it an excellent choice for individuals who are conscious about their dietary choices.

Speedy Cooking: It preheats quickly and cooks food faster than a traditional oven. This is a great time-saving feature, making it suitable for busy households.

Dehydration: You can use the dehydrator function to make healthy snacks like dried fruits, vegetable chips, and beef jerky. This is an excellent way to preserve food without added preservatives.

Easy Cleanup: The non-stick cooking surfaces and dishwasher-safe components make cleanup a breeze, which is especially convenient for those with a busy lifestyle.

Overall, the Ninja Foodi Digital Air Fryer Oven offers the convenience of multiple cooking methods in one appliance while promoting healthier cooking habits by reducing the need for excessive oil. It's a valuable addition to any kitchen for those looking to prepare delicious meals with less hassle and better nutritional value.

TIPS FOR USING IT

Tip 1: Preheat When Necessary

While some recipes may not require preheating, for optimal results, preheat the Air Fryer Oven as directed in your recipe. Preheating helps achieve consistent and even cooking.

Tip 2: Don't Overcrowd the Basket or Trays

Avoid overloading the cooking basket or trays with food. Overcrowding can hinder air circulation and lead to uneven cooking. It's better to cook in batches if necessary.

Tip 3: Apply a Light Oil Spray

When air frying, consider lightly spraying the food with cooking oil or using an oil mister. This can help achieve a crispy texture while minimizing oil usage.

Tip 4: Flip or Shake Midway

For even cooking, flip or shake the contents of the basket or trays halfway through the cooking time. This helps ensure that all sides are cooked uniformly.

Tip 5: Use Parchment Paper or Liners

To simplify cleanup and prevent sticking, consider using parchment paper or silicone liners in the cooking basket or trays. Ensure they are rated safe for air frying.

Tip 6: Prevent Drips and Grease

If you're cooking foods that release a lot of grease, place a tray or foil beneath the cooking basket to catch drips and minimize mess.

Tip 7: Cool Down Safely

After cooking, allow the Air Fryer Oven to cool down before cleaning or storing. The appliance and accessories can be hot immediately after use.

Tip 8: Regular Cleaning

Clean the cooking basket, trays, and interior of the Air Fryer Oven after each use to prevent residue buildup and maintain optimal performance. Refer to the manufacturer's cleaning instructions.

1.Always allow the Ninja Air Fryer to cool down completely after use. The interior and accessories can be very hot, so be careful.

2.Unplug the appliance before starting the cleaning process to ensure safety.

3. Remove all removable attachments, including the cooking basket, cooking tray and any other dishwasher safe parts.

4. Wipe the exterior of the appliance with a damp cloth or sponge. Avoid using abrasive cleaners or scrapers as they can damage the finish.

5. If there are food residues or splatters inside the oven, wipe gently with a damp cloth or sponge.

6. Wash removable accessories in warm, soapy water. Scrub any stubborn residue with a non-abrasive brush or sponge.

7. Empty and clean the drip and crumb trays usually located at the bottom of the oven.

8. If parchment paper or aluminum foil was used during cooking, remove and discard it. Be careful as they can be very hot.

Breakfast

Breakfast

Cherry Almond Scones

Servings: 12
Cooking Time: 25 Minutes
Ingredients:
- 2 3/4 cups all-purpose flour
- 1/2 cup sugar
- 1 tablespoon baking powder
- 3/4 teaspoon salt
- 1 cup dried cherries
- 1 cup slivered almonds
- 1/2 cup cold butter, sliced into tablespoons
- 2 large eggs
- 1/2 cup sour cream
- 1 teaspoon almond extract
- 1/2 teaspoon vanilla extract
- 1 tablespoon milk
- Coarse sugar

Directions:
1. Preheat the toaster oven to 375°F.
2. In a large mixer bowl, stir flour, sugar, baking powder and salt until blended.
3. Add butter pieces. Beat on MEDIUM speed until mixture is crumbly with some larger pieces of butter.
4. In a large mixer bowl on MEDIUM-HIGH speed, beat eggs, sour cream, almond extract and vanilla extract until blended.
5. Stir into flour mixture until mixture is blended and no longer dry. Lightly knead in cherries and almonds.
6. Divide dough in half. Form each into circles about 3/4-inch thick on parchment-lined baking sheet.
7. Brush each circle with milk and sprinkle tops with coarse sugar. Using a floured metal spatula, cut each circle into 6 wedges. Separate the wedges, leaving 1/2-inch between each wedge.
8. Bake for 20 to 25 minutes or until golden brown. Cool for 15 minutes before serving.

Sunny-side Up Eggs

Servings: 2
Cooking Time: 3 Minutes
Ingredients:
- 2 large eggs
- Salt and freshly ground black pepper

Directions:
1. Crack the eggs into an oiled or nonstick small 4 × 8 × 2¼-inch loaf pan. Sprinkle with salt and pepper to taste.
2. TOAST once, or until the eggs are done to your preference.

Flaky Granola

Servings: 3
Cooking Time: 20 Minutes
Ingredients:
- ¼ cup rolled oats
- ½ cup wheat flakes
- ½ cup bran flakes
- ¼ cup wheat germ
- 3 tablespoons sesame seeds
- 4 ¼ cup unsweetened shredded coconut
- ½ cup chopped almonds, walnuts, or pecans
- 2 tablespoons chopped pumpkin seeds
- ½ cup honey or molasses
- 2 tablespoons vegetable oil
- Salt to taste

Directions:
1. Preheat the toaster oven to 375° F.
2. Combine all the ingredients in a medium bowl, stirring to mix well.
3. Spread the mixture in an oiled or nonstick 6½ × 6½ × 2-inch square (cake) pan.
4. BAKE for 20 minutes, turning with tongs every 5 minutes to toast evenly. Cool and store in an airtight container in the refrigerator.

Portobello Burgers

Servings: 4
Cooking Time: 12 Minutes
Ingredients:
- 4 multigrain hamburger buns Dijon mustard
- 4 large portobello mushroom caps, stemmed and brushed clean
- 2 tablespoons olive oil
- Garlic powder
- Salt and butcher's pepper
- 4 thin onion slices
- 4 tomato slices

Directions:
1. TOAST the split hamburger buns and spread each slice with mustard. Set aside.
2. Brush both sides of the mushroom caps with olive oil and sprinkle with garlic powder and salt and pepper to taste.
3. BROIL the caps on a broiling rack with a pan underneath, ribbed side up, for 6 minutes. Turn the mushrooms carefully with tongs and broil again for 6 minutes, or until lightly browned. Place the mushroom caps on the bottom buns and layer each with an onion and tomato slice. Top with the remaining bun halves and serve.

Banana Bread

Servings: 6
Cooking Time: 40 Minutes
Ingredients:
- 2 ripe bananas
- 1 egg
- ½ cup milk
- 2 tablespoons honey
- 2 tablespoons vegetable oil
- ¾ cup chopped trail mix
- 1 cup unbleached flour
- 1 teaspoon baking powder
- Pinch of salt

Directions:
1. Preheat the toaster oven to 400° F.
2. Process the bananas, egg, milk, honey, and oil in a blender or food processor until smooth. Pour into a mixing bowl.
3. Add the flour and trail mix, stirring to mix well. Add the baking powder and salt and stir just enough to blend. Pour the mixture into an oiled or nonstick regular-size 8½ × 4½ × 2¼-inch loaf pan.
4. BAKE for 40 minutes, or until a knife inserted in the center comes out clean.

Wild Blueberry Lemon Chia Bread

Servings: 6
Cooking Time: 27 Minutes
Ingredients:
- ¼ cup extra-virgin olive oil
- ⅓ cup plus 1 tablespoon cane sugar
- 1 large egg
- 3 tablespoons fresh lemon juice
- 1 tablespoon lemon zest
- ⅔ cup milk
- 1 cup all-purpose flour
- ¾ teaspoon baking powder
- ⅛ teaspoon salt
- 2 tablespoons chia seeds
- 1 cup frozen wild blueberries
- ⅓ cup powdered sugar
- 2 teaspoons milk

Directions:
1. Preheat the toaster oven to 310°F.
2. In a medium bowl, mix the olive oil with the sugar. Whisk in the egg, lemon juice, lemon zest, and milk; set aside.
3. In a small bowl, combine the all-purpose flour, baking powder, and salt.
4. Slowly mix the dry ingredients into the wet ingredients. Stir in the chia seeds and wild blueberries.
5. Liberally spray a 7-inch springform pan with olive-oil spray. Pour the batter into the pan and place the pan in the air fryer oven. Bake for 25 to 27 minutes, or until a toothpick inserted in the center comes out clean.
6. Remove and let cool on a wire rack for 10 minutes prior to removing from the pan.
7. Meanwhile, in a small bowl, mix the powdered sugar with the milk to create the glaze.
8. Slice and serve with a drizzle of the powdered sugar glaze.

Italian Strata

Servings: 6
Cooking Time: 55 Minutes
Ingredients:
- 1 cup boiling water
- 3 tablespoons chopped sun-dried tomatoes (dry-packed)
- 5 cups cubed French bread or country bread (cut into 1-inch cubes)
- Nonstick cooking spray
- 1 ½ ounces sliced turkey pepperoni, cut into fourths (about ¾ cup)
- 2 tablespoons chopped pepperoncini peppers
- 1 cup coarsely chopped fresh spinach
- 1 cup shredded Italian blend cheese or mozzarella cheese
- 4 large eggs
- 1 ½ cups whole milk
- 1 teaspoon Italian seasoning
- ¼ teaspoon kosher salt
- 2 tablespoons shredded Parmesan cheese

Directions:
1. Pour the boiling water the over sun-dried tomatoes in a small, deep bowl; set aside.
2. Preheat the toaster oven to 350 °F. Place the bread cubes on a 12 x 12-inch baking pan. Bake for 10 minutes, stirring once.
3. Spray an 8 x 8-inch square baking pan with nonstick cooking spray. Drain the sun-dried tomatoes and pat dry with paper towels. Arrange half the bread cubes evenly in the prepared pan. Top with half the pepperoni, half the pepperoncini, all the spinach, and all of the reconstituted tomatoes. Sprinkle with ½ cup of the Italian cheese. Repeat layers with the remaining bread, pepperoni, pepperoncini, and ½ cup cheese.
4. Whisk the eggs, milk, Italian seasoning, and salt in a large bowl. Pour the egg mixture over the bread layers. Press down lightly with the back of a large spoon. Sprinkle with the Parmesan cheese. Cover and chill for at least 2 hours or overnight.
5. Preheat the toaster oven to 350°F. Bake the strata, uncovered, for 35 to 45 minutes, or until a knife inserted into the center comes out clean. Let stand for 10 minutes before serving.

Bacon Chicken Ranch Sandwiches

Servings: 2
Cooking Time: 23 Minutes
Ingredients:
- Nonstick cooking spray
- ½ pound chicken tenders (about 4)
- 4 slices country or sourdough bread
- 2 tablespoons unsalted or salted butter, softened
- 2 tablespoons ranch dressing
- 2 slices sliced Colby Jack or cheddar cheese
- 6 slices bacon, cooked until crisp

Directions:
1. Preheat the toaster oven to 375°F. Spray a small baking sheet with nonstick cooking spray.
2. Place the chicken tenders on the prepared baking sheet. Bake, uncovered, for 12 to 15 minutes or until the chicken is done and a meat thermometer registers 165°F. Carefully remove from the oven and allow the chicken tenders to cool slightly.
3. Increase the toaster oven temperature to 450°F. Place a 12 x 12-inch baking pan in the toaster oven while it is pre-heating.
4. Spread one side of each slice of bread with butter. Place two pieces of bread, buttered side down, on a sheet of parchment or wax paper. Spread each slice with 1 table-spoon ranch dressing. Divide the chicken tenders among the two slices. Cut the cheese to fit on the chicken tenders and within the bread perimeter. Fold the slices of bacon to fit within the bread perimeter. Top with the second slice of bread, butter side up.
5. Carefully remove the hot baking pan from the toaster oven and place the sandwiches on the baking sheet. Place the baking sheet in the toaster oven and bake for 4 minutes. Carefully remove the pan and flip the sandwich, using a spatula. Bake for an additional 3 to 4 minutes, or until the sandwich is golden brown and the cheese is melted.
6. Cool slightly and cut in half for serving.

Best-ever Cinnamon Rolls

Servings: 10
Cooking Time: 18 Minutes
Ingredients:
- 1 tablespoon unsalted butter, softened
- DOUGH
- ½ cup whole milk
- 2 tablespoons unsalted butter, softened
- 3 tablespoons granulated sugar
- ½ teaspoon table salt
- 1 large egg
- 1 ⅔ cups all-purpose flour, plus more for kneading and dusting
- 1 ¼ teaspoons instant yeast
- FILLING
- ⅔ cup packed dark brown sugar
- 1 tablespoon plus 1 teaspoon ground cinnamon
- Pinch table salt
- 3 tablespoons unsalted butter, melted
- GLAZE
- 1 ½ cups confectioners' sugar
- 1 to 2 tablespoon whole milk
- 1 tablespoon brewed coffee
- ½ teaspoon pure vanilla extract
- 1 tablespoon unsalted butter, melted

Directions:
1. Spread the 1 tablespoon softened butter generously on the sides and bottom of an 8-inch round baking pan.
2. Combine the milk, 2 tablespoons softened butter, sugar, and salt in a 4-cup glass measuring cup. Microwave on High (100 percent) power for 40 seconds or until warm (110°F). (All the butter may not melt.) Whisk in the egg.
3. Stir the flour and yeast in a large bowl. Add the liquid ingredients and stir until you have a soft dough. Flour your hands and a clean surface. Transfer the dough to the floured surface and form it into a ball. Add flour as necessary and knead by pressing the dough with the heel of your hands and turning and repeating. Add just enough flour to keep the dough from being sticky.
4. When the dough is smooth and springs back when you press it with you finger (after 3 to 5 minutes of kneading), place the dough ball into a large oiled bowl, cover with a tea towel, and let rise in a warm place for about an hour or until the dough has almost doubled in size.
5. Transfer the dough to a floured surface and roll into a 10 x 14-inch rectangle.
6. Make the filling: Combine the brown sugar, cinnamon, and salt in a small bowl. Using a pastry brush, brush the melted butter over the entire surface of the dough. Sprinkle the cinnamon-sugar mixture over the butter, using your fingers to lightly press the mixture into the dough. Starting with the longer side, roll up the dough to form a 14-inch cylinder. Gently cut the cylinder into 10 even rolls, using a serrated knife. Place in the prepared pan, cut side up. Cover and let rise in a warm place for about 45 to 60 minutes or until doubled.
7. Preheat the toaster oven to 350°F. Bake for 16 to 18 minutes or until slightly brown on top. Remove from the oven and place on a wire rack.
8. Meanwhile, make the glaze: Whisk the confectioners' sugar, 1 tablespoon milk, the coffee, vanilla, and butter in a medium bowl. If needed, whisk in the additional milk to make the desired consistency. Drizzle over the warm rolls.

Savory Salsa Cheese Rounds

Servings: 6

Cooking Time: 6 Minutes

Ingredients:

- 1 French baguette, cut to make 12
- 1-inch slices (rounds)
- ¼ cup olive oil
- 1 cup Tomato Salsa (recipe follows)
- ½ cup shredded low-fat mozzarella
- 2 tablespoons finely chopped fresh cilantro

Directions:

1. Brush both sides of each round with olive oil.

2. Spread one side of each slice with salsa and sprinkle each with mozzarella. Place the rounds in an oiled or non-stick 8½ × 8½ × 2-inch square baking (cake) pan.

3. BROIL for 6 minutes, or until the cheese is melted and the rounds are lightly browned. Garnish with the chopped cilantro and serve.

Tomato And Artichoke Broiler

Servings: 4

Cooking Time: 10 Minutes

Ingredients:

- 1 small loaf Italian or French bread, sliced in half lengthwise, then quartered
- Filling:
- 2 plum tomatoes, chopped
- 1 5-ounce jar artichokes, drained and chopped
- 2 tablespoons chopped black olives
- 2 tablespoons chopped onion
- 2 garlic cloves, minced
- 2 tablespoons olive oil
- Salt and freshly ground black pepper to taste
- 4 tablespoons grated Parmesan cheese

Directions:

1. Remove enough bread from each quarter to make a small cavity for the sandwich mixture.

2. Combine the filling ingredients and spoon the mixture in equal portions into each of the bread quarter cavities. Sprinkle each quarter with 1 tablespoon Parmesan cheese.

3. BROIL on a broiling rack with a pan underneath for 10 minutes, or until the bread is lightly browned. Slice and serve.

Onion And Cheese Buttermilk Biscuits

Servings: 4

Cooking Time: 15 Minutes

Ingredients:

- 2 cups unbleached flour
- 3 tablespoons margarine, at room temperature
- ¾ cup low-fat buttermilk
- 4 teaspoons baking powder
- 1 teaspoon garlic powder
- ¼ cup grated Parmesan cheese
- 3 tablespoons finely chopped onion
- 2 tablespoons chopped fresh parsley
- Salt to taste

Directions:

1. Preheat the toaster oven to 400° F.

2. Blend all the ingredients in a medium bowl with a fork, then press together to form a dough ball.

3. KNEAD the dough on a lightly floured surface just until smooth.

4. Roll the dough to ½-inch thickness and cut with a round 3-inch cookie cutter. Place on an oiled or nonstick 6½ × 10-inch baking sheet or in an oiled or nonstick 8½ × 8½ × 2-inch square baking (cake) pan.

5. BAKE for 15 minutes, or until lightly browned.

Cinnamon Toast

Servings: 2

Cooking Time: 2 Minutes

Ingredients:

- 1 tablespoon brown sugar
- 2 teaspoons margarine, at room temperature
- ¼ teaspoon ground cinnamon
- 2 slices whole wheat or multigrain bread

Directions:

1. Combine the sugar, margarine, and cinnamon in a small bowl with a fork until well blended. Spread each bread slice with equal portions of the mixture.

2. TOAST once, or until the sugar is melted and the bread is browned to your preference.

English Muffins

Servings: 2

Cooking Time: 4 Minutes

Ingredients:
- 1 English muffin, split
- 1 plum tomato, chopped
- 2 slices reduced-fat or low-fat cheese
- 2 slices reduced-fat honey ham
- 1 tablespoon chopped fresh parsley

Directions:

1. Layer each muffin half with equal portions of tomato, cheese, and ham. Place on a broiling rack with a pan underneath.
2. TOAST once.
3. Garnish each with equal portions of chopped parsley.

French Vegetable Tartines

Servings: 4

Cooking Time: 21 Minutes

Ingredients:
- ½ medium red bell pepper, cut into ½-inch slices
- ½ medium red onion, cut into ½-inch slices
- 2 tablespoons olive oil
- Kosher salt and freshly ground black pepper
- ¾ cup thick-sliced button or white mushrooms
- 8 asparagus spears, trimmed and halved crosswise
- 2 tablespoons unsalted butter, softened
- 1 small clove garlic, minced
- 1 tablespoon minced fresh rosemary leaves
- 4 thick slices French or artisan bread
- ⅓ cup shredded fontina, Gruyère, or Swiss cheese
- Minced fresh flat-leaf (Italian) parsley or thyme leaves

Directions:

1. Preheat the toaster oven to 375°F.
2. Place the red pepper and red onion in a medium bowl. Drizzle with 1 tablespoon of the olive oil and season with salt and pepper; toss to coat well. Arrange the red pepper and onion slices in an ungreased 12 x 12-inch baking pan. Bake, uncovered, for 10 minutes.
3. Place the mushrooms and asparagus pieces in that same bowl. Drizzle with the remaining tablespoon of olive oil and season with salt and pepper. Stir the roasted pepper and onion and add the asparagus and mushrooms to the pan. Bake for 7 to 9 minutes or until the vegetables are tender. Remove the baking pan from the toaster oven and set aside.
4. Meanwhile, stir the butter, garlic, and rosemary in a small bowl. Season with salt and pepper and set aside.
5. Toast the bread in the toaster oven. Spread one side of each slice of toast with the butter mixture. Place the toast, buttered side up, on a baking pan. Arrange the vegetables equally on the toast, then top with the cheese.
6. Preheat the toaster oven on 400°F. Broil the tartines for 1 to 2 minutes, or just until the cheese melts. Garnish with parsley. Serve warm.

Garlic Basil Bread

Servings: 6

Cooking Time: 18 Minutes

Ingredients:
- Mixture:
- 3 tablespoons olive oil
- 2 garlic cloves
- ¼ cup pine nuts (pignoli)
- ½ cup fresh basil leaves
- 2 plum tomatoes, chopped
- Salt to taste
- 1 French baguette, cut diagonally into 1-inch slices

Directions:

1. Preheat the toaster oven to 400° F.
2. Process the mixture ingredients in a blender or food processor until smooth.
3. Spread the mixture on both sides of each bread slice, reassemble into a loaf, and wrap in aluminum foil.
4. BAKE for 12 minutes, or until the bread is thoroughly heated. Peel back the aluminum foil to expose the top of the bread.
5. BAKE again for 5 minutes, or until the top is lightly browned.

Hole In One

Servings: 1

Cooking Time: 7 Minutes

Ingredients:
- 1 slice bread
- 1 teaspoon soft butter
- 1 egg
- salt and pepper
- 1 tablespoon shredded Cheddar cheese
- 2 teaspoons diced ham

Directions:

1. Place a 6 x 6-inch baking dish inside air fryer oven and preheat fryer to 330°F.
2. Using a 2½-inch-diameter biscuit cutter, cut a hole in center of bread slice.
3. Spread softened butter on both sides of bread.
4. Lay bread slice in baking dish and crack egg into the hole. Sprinkle egg with salt and pepper to taste.
5. Air-fry for 5 minutes.
6. Turn toast over and top it with shredded cheese and diced ham.
7. Air-fry for 2 more minutes or until yolk is done to your liking.

Cinnamon Sugar Donut Holes

Servings: 12
Cooking Time: 6 Minutes
Ingredients:
- 1 cup all-purpose flour
- 6 tablespoons cane sugar, divided
- 1 teaspoon baking powder
- 3 teaspoons ground cinnamon, divided
- ¼ teaspoon salt
- 1 large egg
- 1 teaspoon vanilla extract
- 2 tablespoons melted butter

Directions:
1. Preheat the toaster oven to 370°F.
2. In a small bowl, combine the flour, 2 tablespoons of the sugar, the baking powder, 1 teaspoon of the cinnamon, and the salt. Mix well.
3. In a larger bowl, whisk together the egg, vanilla extract, and butter.
4. Slowly add the dry ingredients into the wet until all the ingredients are uniformly combined. Set the bowl inside the refrigerator for at least 30 minutes.
5. Before you're ready to cook, in a small bowl, mix together the remaining 4 tablespoons of sugar and 2 teaspoons of cinnamon.
6. Liberally spray the air fryer oven with olive oil mist so the donut holes don't stick to the bottom.
7. Remove the dough from the refrigerator and divide it into 12 equal donut holes. You can use a 1-ounce serving scoop if you have one.
8. Roll each donut hole in the sugar and cinnamon mixture; then place in the air fryer oven. Repeat until all the donut holes are covered in the sugar and cinnamon mixture.
9. When the oven is full, air-fry for 6 minutes. Remove the donut holes from the oven using oven-safe tongs and let cool 5 minutes. Repeat until all 12 are cooked.

Sheet-pan Hash Browns

Servings: 2
Cooking Time: 60 Minutes
Ingredients:
- 1½ pounds Yukon Gold potatoes, unpeeled, shredded
- 3 tablespoons extra-virgin olive oil
- ½ teaspoon table salt
- ⅛ teaspoon pepper

Directions:
1. Adjust toaster oven rack to lowest position, select air-fry or convection function, and preheat the toaster oven to 450 degrees. Place potatoes in large bowl and cover with cold water. Let sit for 5 minutes.
2. Lift potatoes out of water, one handful at a time, and transfer to colander; discard water. Rinse and dry bowl. Place half of shredded potatoes in center of clean dish towel. Gather ends of towel and twist tightly to wring out excess moisture from potatoes. Transfer dried potatoes to now-empty bowl. Repeat with remaining potatoes.
3. Add oil, salt, and pepper to potatoes and toss to combine. Distribute potatoes in even layer on small rimmed baking sheet, but do not pack down. Cook until top of potatoes is spotty brown, 30 to 40 minutes, rotating sheet halfway through baking.
4. Remove sheet from oven. Using spatula, flip hash browns in sections. Return sheet to oven and continue to cook until spotty brown and dry, 10 to 15 minutes. Season with salt and pepper to taste. Serve.

Buttermilk Pancakes

Servings: 4
Cooking Time: 20 Minutes
Ingredients:
- Batter:
- 1 cup low-fat buttermilk
- 1 egg
- 1 cup unbleached flour
- 3 tablespoons wheat germ
- 1 tablespoon honey
- 1 tablespoon olive oil
- Salt to taste
- 1 teaspoon baking powder
- 1 tablespoon olive oil for brushing pan
- Honey, maple syrup, or molasses

Directions:
1. Blend the batter ingredients in a food processor or blender until smooth. Stir in the baking powder. Pour enough batter into an oiled or nonstick 9½-inch-diameter round cake pan to make the size pancake you prefer.
2. BROIL 5 minutes, or until the batter pulls away from the sides and starts browning. Remove the pan from the oven and, with a spatula, turn the pancake over.
3. BROIL again for 5 minutes, or until the pancake is lightly browned. Transfer to a plate and repeat the broiling steps for the remaining batter. Serve with honey, maple syrup, or molasses.

Fry Bread

Servings: 4
Cooking Time: 5 Minutes
Ingredients:
- 1 cup flour
- 2 teaspoons baking powder
- ¼ teaspoon salt
- ¼ cup lukewarm milk
- 1 teaspoon oil
- 2–3 tablespoons water
- oil for misting or cooking spray

Directions:

1. Stir together flour, baking powder, and salt. Gently mix in the milk and oil. Stir in 1 tablespoon water. If needed, add more water 1 tablespoon at a time until stiff dough forms. Dough shouldn't be sticky, so use only as much as you need.

2. Divide dough into 4 portions and shape into balls. Cover with a towel and let rest for 10 minutes.

3. Preheat the toaster oven to 390°F.

4. Shape dough as desired:

5. a. Pat into 3-inch circles. This will make a thicker bread to eat plain or with a sprinkle of cinnamon or honey butter. You can cook all 4 at once.

6. b. Pat thinner into rectangles about 3 x 6 inches. This will create a thinner bread to serve as a base for dishes such as Indian tacos. The circular shape is more traditional, but rectangles allow you to cook 2 at a time in your air fryer oven.

7. Spray both sides of dough pieces with oil or cooking spray.

8. Place the 4 circles or 2 of the dough rectangles in the air fryer oven and air-fry at 390°F for 3 minutes. Spray tops, turn, spray other side, and air fry for 2 more minutes. If necessary, repeat to cook remaining bread.

9. Serve piping hot as is or allow to cool slightly and add toppings to create your own Native American tacos.

Strawberry Bread

Servings: 6
Cooking Time: 28 Minutes
Ingredients:
- ½ cup frozen strawberries in juice, completely thawed (do not drain)
- 1 cup flour
- ½ cup sugar
- 1 teaspoon cinnamon
- ½ teaspoon baking soda
- ⅛ teaspoon salt
- 1 egg, beaten
- ⅓ cup oil
- cooking spray

Directions:
1. Cut any large berries into smaller pieces no larger than ½ inch.
2. Preheat the toaster oven to 330°F.
3. In a large bowl, stir together the flour, sugar, cinnamon, soda, and salt.
4. In a small bowl, mix together the egg, oil, and strawberries. Add to dry ingredients and stir together gently.
5. Spray 6 x 6-inch baking pan with cooking spray.
6. Pour batter into prepared pan and air-fry at 330°F for 28 minutes.
7. When bread is done, let cool for 10 minutes before removing from pan.

Autumn Berry Dessert

Servings: 4
Cooking Time: 5 Minutes
Ingredients:
- ½ cup nonfat sour cream
- ½ cup nonfat plain yogurt
- 3 tablespoons brown sugar
- 1 16-ounce package frozen blueberries or
- 2 cups fresh blueberries, rinsed well and drained
- 1 16-ounce package frozen sliced strawberries or 2 cups sliced fresh strawberries
- 4 tablespoons ground walnuts or pecans
- Grated lemon zest

Directions:
1. Beat together the sour cream, yogurt, and brown sugar in a small bowl with an electric mixer until smooth. Set aside.
2. Combine the berries in an oilcd or nonstick 8½ × 8½ × 2-inch square baking (cake) pan.
3. BROIL for 5 minutes, or until bubbling. Fill 4 individual 1-cup-size ovenproof dishes with equal portions of the berries and top with the yogurt/sour cream mixture. Serve immediately or reheat by broiling for 1 or 2 minutes prior to serving. Sprinkle each serving with a tablespoon of ground walnuts or a pinch of lemon zest.

Strawberry Pie Glaze

Servings: 2
Cooking Time: 15 Minutes
Ingredients:
- ½ cup apple juice
- 2 tablespoons sugar
- 1 teaspoon lemon or lime juice

Directions:
1. Combine all the ingredients in an oiled or nonstick 8½ × 8½ × 2-inch square baking (cake) pan.
2. BROIL for 6 minutes, or until the sugar is melted. Carefully remove from the oven using oven mitts, stir to blend, then broil again for 6 minutes, or until the liquid is reduced and clear. Remove from the oven and brush the strawberries immediately with the glaze. Chill before serving.

Rosemary Bread

Servings: 6
Cooking Time: 15 Minutes
Ingredients:
- Spread:
- 3 tablespoons olive oil
- 2 tablespoons margarine
- 1 teaspoon garlic
- 2 tablespoons grated Parmesan cheese
- 3 1 tablespoon finely chopped fresh rosemary leaves
- ½ teaspoon freshly ground black pepper

- Salt to taste
- 1 French baguette, sliced 2 inches thick

Directions:
1. Preheat the toaster oven to 350° F.
2. Combine the spread ingredients in a small bowl, blending well with a fork. Adjust the seasonings to taste.
3. Spread the mixture on both sides of the bread slices and wrap the loaf in aluminum foil.
4. BAKE for 10 minutes. Remove from the oven and peel back the foil, exposing the top of the bread loaf. Bake for another 5 minutes, or until the top is lightly browned.

Sheet Pan French Toast

Servings: 2
Cooking Time: 15 Minutes

Ingredients:
- Oil spray (hand-pumped)
- 2 large eggs
- ¼ cup milk
- 1 teaspoon vanilla extract
- ¼ teaspoon ground cinnamon
- 4 slices whole-grain bread
- ¾ cup maple syrup, or to taste

Directions:
1. Preheat the toaster oven on BAKE to 350°F for 5 minutes.
2. Line the baking tray with parchment paper and generously spray the paper with oil.
3. In a medium bowl, whisk the eggs, milk, vanilla, and cinnamon until well blended.
4. Dredge a slice of bread in the egg mixture until submerged, turn, and take it out. Gently shake the bread to remove any excess egg mixture and place the bread on the baking sheet. Repeat with the remaining bread.
5. Bake for 10 minutes.
6. Flip the bread and bake for 5 minutes longer until both sides are golden brown and crispy.
7. Serve with maple syrup.

Blueberry Lemon Muffins

Servings: 12
Cooking Time: 23 Minutes

Ingredients:
- 2 ¼ cups all-purpose flour
- 1 ½ cups fresh blueberries
- 3/4 cup granulated sugar
- 2 teaspoons baking powder
- ½ teaspoon lemon zest
- ½ teaspoon salt
- ¾ cup milk
- ¼ cup butter, melted
- 1 tablespoon lemon juice
- 1 large egg

Directions:
1. Preheat the toaster oven to 375°F. Grease or line a 12-cup muffin pan with paper baking cups. Set aside.
2. In a large bowl, stir together flour, blueberries, granulated sugar, baking powder and salt.
3. In a small bowl, using an electric mixer or whisk, beat milk, butter, lemon juice and egg until blended.
4. Gradually add milk mixture to flour mixture. Stir until just blended.
5. Spoon into prepared muffin pan.
6. Bake 20 to 23 minutes or until toothpick inserted in center comes out clean.

Strawberry Shortcake With Buttermilk Biscuits

Servings: 8
Cooking Time: 15 Minutes

Ingredients:
- 1 quart fresh strawberries, rinsed and sliced
- 2 tablespoons sugar
- 1 tablespoon lemon juice
- Buttermilk biscuit mix:
- 2 cups unbleached flour
- 2 teaspoons baking powder
- ½ teaspoon baking soda
- Salt to taste
- ¼ cup margarine
- 1 cup low-fat buttermilk
- Vegetable oil
- Nonfat whipped topping

Directions:
1. Preheat the toaster oven to 400° F.
2. Combine the strawberries, sugar, and lemon juice in a large bowl, mixing well to blend. Set aside.
3. Combine the flour, baking powder, baking soda, and salt in a large bowl. Add the margarine, cutting it into the flour with a knife or pastry cutter. Add just enough buttermilk so that the dough will hold together when pinched.
4. Turn the dough out onto a lightly floured surface and knead 5 or 6 times. Drop the dough from a tablespoon onto an oiled or nonstick 6½ × 10-inch baking sheet. Make 8 mounds 1½ inches across and flatten the tops with a spoon.
5. BAKE for 15 minutes, or until the biscuits are lightly browned. Cool. Spoon on the fresh strawberries. Top with nonfat whipped topping and serve.

Salmon Burgers

Servings: 4
Cooking Time: 25 Minutes
Ingredients:
- ¾ cup Homemade Bread Crumbs
- 1 15-ounce can salmon, drained
- 1 small zucchini, finely chopped
- 2 tablespoons finely chopped onions
- 1 egg
- 1 teaspoon dried rosemary
- 1 teaspoon lemon juice
- 1 teaspoon garlic powder
- Salt and freshly ground black pepper to taste
- 1 teaspoon vegetable oil

Directions:
1. Preheat the toaster oven to 400° F.
2. Blend all ingredients except the oil and form patties 1½ inches thick. Place on an oiled or nonstick 8½ × 8½ × 2-inch square baking (cake) pan.
3. BAKE for 25 minutes, or until the patties are lightly browned.

Smoked Turkey, Walnut, And Pimiento Sandwich

Servings: 2
Cooking Time: 4 Minutes
Ingredients:
- Mixture:
- Stone-ground mustard
- 2 tablespoons canned diced pimientos
- 2 tablespoons finely chopped scallions
- 2 tablespoons finely chopped walnuts
- 2 tablespoons chopped raisins
- ½ teaspoon dill
- 2 tablespoons reduced-fat mayonnaise
- Salt and butcher's pepper to taste
- 4 slices rye bread
- 1 2.5-ounce package smoked turkey breast slices

Directions:
1. Combine the mixture ingredients and spread in equal portions on all bread slices. Layer 2 bread slices with equal portions of smoked turkey breast. Top with the other bread slices to make sandwiches.
2. TOAST twice on a broiling rack with a pan underneath.

Banana Baked Oatmeal

Servings: 4
Cooking Time: 35 Minutes
Ingredients:
- Oil spray (hand-pumped)
- 1 cup rolled gluten-free oats
- ¾ teaspoon baking powder
- ¾ teaspoon ground cinnamon
- ¼ teaspoon sea salt
- ¾ cup whole milk
- ¼ cup maple syrup
- 1 large egg
- 2 tablespoons unsalted butter, melted
- 1 teaspoon vanilla extract
- 1 banana, chopped

Directions:
1. Place the rack on position 1 and preheat the toaster oven on BAKE to 375°F for 5 minutes.
2. Lightly spray an 8-inch-square baking dish with oil and set aside.
3. In a large bowl, stir the oats, baking powder, cinnamon, and salt until well combined.
4. In a small bowl, whisk the milk, maple syrup, egg, butter, and vanilla until blended.
5. Add the wet ingredients to the dry and stir until well mixed. Stir in the banana.
6. Spoon the batter into the baking dish and place the wire rack on position 1.
7. Place the baking dish on the rack and bake for 35 minutes. The oatmeal should look just set in the middle; if not, add 5 minutes more.
8. Cool the baked oatmeal for 5 minutes and serve with desired toppings.

Snacks Appetizers And Sides

Snacks Appetizers And Sides

Cuban Sliders

Servings: 8
Cooking Time: 8 Minutes

Ingredients:
- 8 slices ciabatta bread, ¼-inch thick
- cooking spray
- 1 tablespoon brown mustard
- 6-8 ounces thin sliced leftover roast pork
- 4 ounces thin deli turkey
- ⅓ cup bread and butter pickle slices
- 2–3 ounces Pepper Jack cheese slices

Directions:
1. Spray one side of each slice of bread with butter or olive oil cooking spray.
2. Spread brown mustard on other side of each slice.
3. Layer pork roast, turkey, pickles, and cheese on 4 of the slices. Top with remaining slices.
4. Air-fry at 390°F for approximately 8 minutes. The sandwiches should be golden brown.
5. Cut each slider in half to make 8 portions.

Broiled Maryland Crabcakes With Creamy Herb Sauce

Servings: 8-9
Cooking Time: 8 Minutes

Ingredients:
- 1 large egg
- 3 Tablespoons mayonnaise
- 1 Tablespoon brown mustard
- 1 Tablespoon all-purpose flour
- 1 teaspoon seafood seasoning
- 1/2 teasoon salt
- 1/4 teaspoon ground black pepper
- 1 pound lump crabmeat
- 1/4 cup chopped parsley
- 1 small shallot, minced
- 1 garlic clove, minced
- Creamy Herb Sauce

Directions:
1. In a medium bowl, mix egg, mayonnaise, mustard, flour, seafood seasoning, salt and pepper until well blended.
2. Stir in crabmeat, parsley, shallots and garlic until crab is coated with mayonnaise mixture.
3. Place 1/4 cup crab mixture on broiler pan; lightly press down. Repeat with remaining mixture.
4. Set toaster oven on BROIL. Broil crabcakes 8 minutes, without turning.
5. Serve with Creamy Herb Sauce.

Garlic Wings

Servings: 4
Cooking Time: 15 Minutes

Ingredients:
- 2 pounds chicken wings
- oil for misting
- cooking spray
- Marinade
- 1 cup buttermilk
- 2 cloves garlic, mashed flat
- 1 teaspoon Worcestershire sauce
- 1 bay leaf
- Coating
- 1½ cups grated Parmesan cheese
- ¾ cup breadcrumbs
- 1½ tablespoons garlic powder
- ½ teaspoon salt

Directions:
1. Mix all marinade ingredients together.
2. Remove wing tips (the third joint) and discard or freeze for stock. Cut the remaining wings at the joint and toss them into the marinade, stirring to coat well. Refrigerate for at least an hour but no more than 8 hours.
3. When ready to cook, combine all coating ingredients in a shallow dish.
4. Remove wings from marinade, shaking off excess, and roll in coating mixture. Press coating into wings so that it sticks well. Spray wings with oil.
5. Spray air fryer oven with cooking spray. Place wings in air fryer oven in single layer, close but not touching.
6. Air-fry at 360°F for 15 minutes or until chicken is done and juices run clear.
7. Repeat previous step to cook remaining wings.

Cauliflower "tater" Tots

Servings: 6
Cooking Time: 10 Minutes

Ingredients:
- 1 head of cauliflower
- 2 eggs
- ¼ cup all-purpose flour
- ½ cup grated Parmesan cheese
- 1 teaspoon salt
- freshly ground black pepper
- vegetable or olive oil, in a spray bottle

Directions:

1. Grate the head of cauliflower with a box grater or finely chop it in a food processor. You should have about 3½ cups. Place the chopped cauliflower in the center of a clean kitchen towel and twist the towel tightly to squeeze all the water out of the cauliflower. (This can be done in two batches to make it easier to drain all the water from the cauliflower.)

2. Place the squeezed cauliflower in a large bowl. Add the eggs, flour, Parmesan cheese, salt and freshly ground black pepper. Shape the cauliflower into small cylinders or "tater tot" shapes, rolling roughly one tablespoon of the mixture at a time. Place the tots on a cookie sheet lined with paper towel to absorb any residual moisture. Spray the cauliflower tots all over with oil.

3. Preheat the toaster oven to 400°F.

4. Air-fry the tots at 400°F, one layer at a time for 10 minutes, turning them over for the last few minutes of the cooking process for even browning. Season with salt and black pepper. Serve hot with your favorite dipping sauce.

Garden Fresh Bruschetta

Servings: 6
Cooking Time: 5 Minutes

Ingredients:
- 1/2 cup Parmigiano-Reggiano cheese
- 2 cloves garlic (or to taste)
- 2 tablespoons balsamic vinegar
- 1/3 cup pine nuts
- 1 loaf crusty Italian bread
- 1 or 2 fresh tomatoes, sliced or chopped
- Salt and pepper to taste
- 4 cups fresh basil leaves, stems removed

Directions:

1. With shredding disk inserted, shred cheese in food processor. Remove from food processor and set aside.

2. Insert S-blade in food processor and coarsely chop basil leaves and garlic. Add vinegar and pulse a few times. Add pine nuts to basil mixture and pulse until coarsely chopped. With food processor running, drizzle olive oil through feed chute until ingredients are coated and spreadable. Add half of the already grated Parmesan cheese and pulse until just blended.

3. To assemble: Slice crusty bread on diagonal, place on toaster oven size cookie sheet. On each piece of bread, spread basil mixture. Place tomatoes on top of basil, add salt and pepper to taste. Sprinkle some of the remaining cheese on top.

4. Place in preheated 350°F toaster oven for 5 minutes or until cheese melts and bread is warmed. Serve as an appetizer.

Shrimp Pirogues

Servings: 8
Cooking Time: 5 Minutes

Ingredients:
- 12 ounces small, peeled, and deveined raw shrimp
- 3 ounces cream cheese, room temperature
- 2 tablespoons plain yogurt
- 1 teaspoon lemon juice
- 1 teaspoon dried dill weed, crushed
- salt
- 4 small hothouse cucumbers, each approximately 6 inches long

Directions:

1. Pour 4 tablespoons water in bottom of air fryer oven.

2. Place shrimp in air fryer oven in single layer and air-fry at 390°F for 5 minutes, just until done. Watch carefully because shrimp cooks quickly, and overcooking makes it tough.

3. Chop shrimp into small pieces, no larger than ½ inch. Refrigerate while mixing the remaining ingredients.

4. With a fork, mash and whip the cream cheese until smooth.

5. Stir in the yogurt and beat until smooth. Stir in lemon juice, dill weed, and chopped shrimp.

6. Taste for seasoning. If needed, add ¼ to ½ teaspoon salt to suit your taste.

7. Store in refrigerator until serving time.

8. When ready to serve, wash and dry cucumbers and split them lengthwise. Scoop out the seeds and turn cucumbers upside down on paper towels to drain for 10 minutes.

9. Just before filling, wipe centers of cucumbers dry. Spoon the shrimp mixture into the pirogues and cut in half crosswise. Serve immediately.

Avocado Fries, Vegan

Servings: 4
Cooking Time: 10 Minutes
Ingredients:
- ¼ cup almond or coconut milk
- 1 tablespoon lime juice
- ⅛ teaspoon hot sauce
- 2 tablespoons flour
- ¾ cup panko breadcrumbs
- ¼ cup cornmeal
- ¼ teaspoon salt
- 1 large avocado
- oil for misting or cooking spray

Directions:
1. In a small bowl, whisk together the almond or coconut milk, lime juice, and hot sauce.
2. Place flour on a sheet of wax paper.
3. Mix panko, cornmeal, and salt and place on another sheet of wax paper.
4. Split avocado in half and remove pit. Peel or use a spoon to lift avocado halves out of the skin.
5. Cut avocado lengthwise into ½-inch slices. Dip each in flour, then milk mixture, then roll in panko mixture.
6. Mist with oil or cooking spray and air-fry at 390°F for 10 minutes, until crust is brown and crispy.

Hot Bacon-cheese Dip

Servings: 3
Cooking Time: 30 Minutes
Ingredients:
- Nonstick cooking spray
- 1 (8-ounce) package cream cheese, cut into cubes and softened
- 1 cup sour cream
- 2 tablespoons whole milk
- 1 tablespoon Worcestershire sauce
- ¼ teaspoon Sriracha or hot sauce
- 10 strips bacon, cooked until crisp and crumbled
- 8 ounces shredded sharp cheddar cheese
- 1 green onion, white and green portions, thinly sliced
- Tortilla chips, crackers, broccoli or cauliflower florets, or other favorites, for dipping

Directions:
1. Preheat the toaster oven to 350°F. Spray a 1-quart casserole dish with nonstick cooking spray.
2. Stir the cream cheese, sour cream, milk, Worcestershire sauce, and Sriracha in a medium bowl. Blend well.
3. Reserve 2 tablespoon crumbled bacon for the garnish. Stir the remaining bacon and the cheddar cheese into the cream cheese mixture. Spoon into the prepared dish and cover.
4. Bake for 20 minutes. Stir the dip, cover, and bake for an additional 10 minutes or until hot and melted. Garnish with the reserved bacon and green onion.
5. Serve warm with any of your favorites for dipping.

Sesame Green Beans

Servings: 4
Cooking Time: 8 Minutes
Ingredients:
- 1 pound green beans, stems trimmed
- 1 tablespoon olive oil
- 1 teaspoon sesame oil
- 1 tablespoon sesame seeds
- Pinch sea salt

Directions:
1. Preheat the toaster oven to 350°F on AIR FRY for 5 minutes.
2. In a large bowl, toss the green beans, olive oil, and sesame oil.
3. Place the air-fryer basket in the baking tray and spread the beans in the basket.
4. Place the tray in position 2 and air fry for 8 minutes, shaking the basket at the halfway point. The beans should be lightly golden and fragrant.
5. Transfer the beans to a serving plate and serve topped with the sesame seeds and seasoned with salt.

Skinny Fries

Servings: 2
Cooking Time: 15 Minutes
Ingredients:
- 2 to 3 russet potatoes, peeled and cut into ¼-inch sticks
- 2 to 3 teaspoons olive or vegetable oil
- salt

Directions:
1. Cut the potatoes into ¼-inch strips. (A mandolin with a julienne blade is really helpful here.) Rinse the potatoes with cold water several times and let them soak in cold water for at least 10 minutes or as long as overnight.
2. Preheat the toaster oven to 380°F.
3. Drain and dry the potato sticks really well, using a clean kitchen towel. Toss the fries with the oil in a bowl and then air-fry the fries in two batches at 380°F for 15 minutes.
4. Add the first batch of French fries back into the air fryer oven with the finishing batch and let everything warm through for a few minutes. As soon as the fries are done, season them with salt and transfer to a plate. Serve them warm with ketchup or your favorite dip.

Mustard Green Beans With Walnuts

Servings: 4
Cooking Time: 20 Minutes
Ingredients:
- 1 ½ pounds fresh green beans, trimmed
- Nonstick cooking spray
- Kosher salt and freshly ground black pepper
- 1 ½ tablespoons white wine vinegar
- 2 tablespoons finely chopped shallots
- 1 ½ tablespoons Dijon mustard
- 1 teaspoon honey
- 2 tablespoons extra-virgin olive oil
- ⅓ cup coarsely chopped walnuts, toasted

Directions:
1. Preheat the toaster oven to 425°F. Place the green beans in a large bowl and spray with nonstick cooking spray. Season with salt and pepper. Place the green beans in a 12 x 12-inch baking pan.
2. Roast for 10 minutes. Stir and roast for an additional 10 minutes, or until the green beans are the desired tenderness.
3. Meanwhile, whisk the vinegar and shallots in a large bowl. Let stand while the green beans are roasting. Whisk the mustard into the vinegar mixture. Stir in the honey. Gradually add the olive oil, whisking until the mixture is thick. Add the green beans; toss gently to coat. Season to taste with additional salt and pepper, if needed. Sprinkle with the walnuts. Serve at room temperature.

Baked Spicy Pimento Cheese Dip

Servings: 20
Cooking Time: 45 Minutes
Ingredients:
- 1 jar (4 oz.) sweet pimentos, drained
- 8 ounces block of cheddar cheese, shredded
- 2 Tablespoons hot sauce
- 2 teaspoons jarred garlic (or 2 whole cloves)
- 1/4 cup chopped onion
- 1/2 cup mayonnaise
- 1/2 teaspoon salt
- 1/2 teaspoon pepper
- 8 ounces cream cheese

Directions:
1. Preheat toaster oven to 350 degrees.
2. Combine all ingredients in a large bowl, then mix well using a hand blender, food processor or hand mixer.
3. Transfer cheese mixture into a shallow metal baking dish (8x8).
4. Place into toaster oven and bake for 40-45 minutes, or until edges are golden brown and bubbling.

Buffalo Bites

Servings: 16
Cooking Time: 12 Minutes
Ingredients:
- 1 pound ground chicken
- 8 tablespoons buffalo wing sauce
- 2 ounces Gruyère cheese, cut into 16 cubes
- 1 tablespoon maple syrup

Directions:
1. Mix 4 tablespoons buffalo wing sauce into all the ground chicken.
2. Shape chicken into a log and divide into 16 equal portions.
3. With slightly damp hands, mold each chicken portion around a cube of cheese and shape into a firm ball. When you have shaped 8 meatballs, place them in air fryer oven.
4. Air-fry at 390°F for approximately 5 minutes. Reduce temperature to 360°F, and air-fry for 5 minutes longer.
5. While the first batch is cooking, shape remaining chicken and cheese into 8 more meatballs.
6. Repeat step 4 to cook second batch of meatballs.
7. In a medium bowl, mix the remaining 4 tablespoons of buffalo wing sauce with the maple syrup. Add all the cooked meatballs and toss to coat.
8. Place meatballs back into air fryer oven and air-fry at 390°F for 2 minutes to set the glaze. Skewer each with a toothpick and serve.

Crispy Spiced Chickpeas

Servings: 4
Cooking Time: 12 Minutes
Ingredients:
- 1 (15 ounce) can chickpeas, drained, rinsed, and patted dry
- 1 tablespoon olive oil
- ½ teaspoon cumin
- ¼ teaspoon paprika
- ½ teaspoon ground fennel seeds
- ⅛ teaspoon cayenne pepper

Directions:
1. Combine all ingredients in a large bowl and stir to combine.
2. Preheat the toaster oven to 430°F.
3. Place chickpeas on the food tray, then insert the tray at mid position in the preheated oven.
4. Select the Air Fry function, adjust time to 12 minutes, and press Start/Pause.
5. Remove when chickpeas are crispy and golden.

Dill Fried Pickles With Light Ranch Dip

Servings: 4
Cooking Time: 8 Minutes
Ingredients:
- 4 to 6 large dill pickles, sliced in half or quartered lengthwise
- ½ cup all-purpose flour
- 2 eggs, lightly beaten
- 1 cup plain breadcrumbs
- 1 teaspoon salt
- ⅛ teaspoon cayenne pepper
- 2 tablespoons fresh dill leaves, dried well
- vegetable oil, in a spray bottle
- Light Ranch Dip
- ¼ cup reduced-fat mayonnaise
- ¼ cup buttermilk
- ¼ cup non-fat Greek yogurt
- 1 tablespoon chopped fresh chives
- 1 tablespoon chopped fresh parsley
- 1 tablespoon lemon juice
- salt and freshly ground black pepper

Directions:
1. Dry the dill pickle spears very well with a clean kitchen towel.
2. Set up a dredging station using three shallow dishes. Place the flour in the first shallow dish. Place the eggs into the second dish. Combine the breadcrumbs, salt, cayenne and fresh dill in a food processor and process until everything is combined and the crumbs are very fine. Place the crumb mixture in the third dish.
3. Preheat the toaster oven to 400°F.
4. Coat the pickles by dredging them first in the flour, then the egg, and then the breadcrumbs, pressing the crumbs on gently with your hands. Set the coated pickles on a tray and spray them on all sides with vegetable oil.
5. Air-fry one layer of pickles at a time at 400°F for 8 minutes, turning them over halfway through the cooking process and spraying lightly again if necessary. The crumbs should be nicely browned on all sides.
6. While the pickles are air-frying, make the light ranch dip by mixing everything together in a bowl. Serve the pickles warm with the dip on the side.

Middle Eastern Phyllo Rolls

Servings: 6
Cooking Time: 5 Minutes
Ingredients:
- 6 ounces Lean ground beef or ground lamb
- 3 tablespoons Sliced almonds
- 1 tablespoon Chutney (any variety), finely chopped
- ¼ teaspoon Ground cinnamon
- ¼ teaspoon Ground coriander
- ¼ teaspoon Ground cumin
- ¼ teaspoon Ground dried turmeric
- ¼ teaspoon Table salt
- ¼ teaspoon Ground black pepper
- 6 18 × 14-inch phyllo sheets (thawed, if necessary)
- Olive oil spray

Directions:
1. Set a medium skillet over medium heat for a minute or two, then crumble in the ground meat. Air-fry for 3 minutes, stirring often, or until well browned. Stir in the almonds, chutney, cinnamon, coriander, cumin, turmeric, salt, and pepper until well combined. Remove from the heat, scrape the cooked ground meat mixture into a bowl, and cool for 15 minutes.
2. Preheat the toaster oven to 400°F.
3. Place one sheet of phyllo dough on a clean, dry work surface. (Keep the others covered.) Lightly coat it with olive oil spray, then fold it in half by bringing the short ends together. Place about 3 tablespoons of the ground meat mixture along one of the longer edges, then fold both of the shorter sides of the dough up and over the meat to partially enclose it (and become a border along the sheet of dough). Roll the dough closed, coat it with olive oil spray on all sides, and set it aside seam side down. Repeat this filling and spraying process with the remaining phyllo sheets.
4. Set the rolls seam side down in the air fryer oven in one layer with some air space between them. Air-fry undisturbed for 5 minutes, or until very crisp and golden brown.
5. Use kitchen tongs to transfer the rolls to a wire rack. Cool for only 2 or 3 minutes before serving hot.

Parmesan Peas

Servings: 3
Cooking Time: 15 Minutes
Ingredients:
- 3 tablespoons olive oil
- 1 clove garlic, minced
- 1 1/2 cups frozen peas, thawed and drained
- 1/2 cup shredded Parmesan cheese
- 1/2 teaspoon coarse pepper

Directions:
1. Heat the toaster oven to 350°F.
2. In toaster oven baking pan, add oil and garlic.
3. Bake for 5 minutes or until garlic is lightly browned.
4. Add peas to the pan.
5. Bake an additional 8 to 10 minutes or until peas are heated.
6. Sprinkle with cheese and pepper before serving.

Grilled Ham & Muenster Cheese On Raisin Bread

Servings: 1
Cooking Time: 10 Minutes
Ingredients:
• 2 slices raisin bread
• 2 tablespoons butter, softened
• 2 teaspoons honey mustard
• 3 slices thinly sliced honey ham (about 3 ounces)
• 4 slices Muenster cheese (about 3 ounces)
• 2 toothpicks
Directions:
1. Preheat the toaster oven to 370°F.
2. Spread the softened butter on one side of both slices of raisin bread and place the bread, buttered side down on the counter. Spread the honey mustard on the other side of each slice of bread. Layer 2 slices of cheese, the ham and the remaining 2 slices of cheese on one slice of bread and top with the other slice of bread. Remember to leave the buttered side of the bread on the outside.
3. Transfer the sandwich to the air fryer oven and secure the sandwich with toothpicks.
4. Air-fry at 370°F for 5 minutes. Flip the sandwich over, remove the toothpicks and air-fry for another 5 minutes. Cut the sandwich in half and enjoy!!

Pork Pot Stickers With Yum Yum Sauce

Servings: 48
Cooking Time: 8 Minutes
Ingredients:
• 1 pound ground pork
• 2 cups shredded green cabbage
• ¼ cup shredded carrot
• ½ cup finely chopped water chestnuts
• 2 teaspoons minced fresh ginger
• ¼ cup hoisin sauce
• 2 tablespoons soy sauce
• 1 tablespoon sesame oil
• freshly ground black pepper
• 3 scallions, minced
• 48 round dumpling wrappers (or wonton wrappers with the corners cut off to make them round)
• 1 tablespoon vegetable oil
• soy sauce, for serving
• Yum Yum Sauce:
• 1½ cups mayonnaise
• 2 tablespoons sugar
• 3 tablespoons rice vinegar
• 1 teaspoon soy sauce
• 2 tablespoons ketchup
• 1½ teaspoons paprika
• ¼ teaspoon ground cayenne pepper
• ¼ teaspoon garlic powder
Directions:
1. Preheat a large sauté pan over medium-high heat. Add the ground pork and brown for a few minutes. Remove the cooked pork to a bowl using a slotted spoon and discard the fat from the pan. Return the cooked pork to the sauté pan and add the cabbage, carrots and water chestnuts. Sauté for a minute and then add the fresh ginger, hoisin sauce, soy sauce, sesame oil, and freshly ground black pepper. Sauté for a few more minutes, just until cabbage and carrots are soft. Then stir in the scallions and transfer the pork filling to a bowl to cool.
2. Make the pot stickers in batches of 1 Place 12 dumpling wrappers on a flat surface. Brush a little water around the perimeter of the wrappers. Place a rounded teaspoon of the filling into the center of each wrapper. Fold the wrapper over the filling, bringing the edges together to form a half moon, sealing the edges shut. Brush a little more water on the top surface of the sealed edge of the pot sticker. Make pleats in the dough around the sealed edge by pinching the dough and folding the edge over on itself. You should have about 5 to 6 pleats in the dough. Repeat this three times until you have 48 pot stickers. Freeze the pot stickers for 2 hours (or as long as 3 weeks in an airtight container).
3. Preheat the toaster oven to 400°F.
4. Air-fry the pot stickers in batches of 16. Brush or spray the pot stickers with vegetable oil just before putting them in the air fryer oven. Air-fry for 8 minutes, turning the pot stickers once or twice during the cooking process.
5. While the pot stickers are cooking, combine all the ingredients for the Yum Yum sauce in a bowl. Serve the pot stickers warm with the Yum Yum sauce and soy sauce for dipping.

Crispy Wontons

Servings: 8
Cooking Time: 10 Minutes
Ingredients:
• ½ cup refried beans
• 3 tablespoons salsa
• ¼ cup canned artichoke hearts, drained and patted dry
• ¼ cup frozen spinach, defrosted and squeezed dry
• 2 ounces cream cheese
• 1½ teaspoons dried oregano, divided
• ¼ teaspoon garlic powder
• ¼ teaspoon onion powder
• ½ teaspoon salt
• ¼ cup chopped pepperoni
• ¼ cup grated mozzarella cheese
• 1 tablespoon grated Parmesan
• 2 ounces cream cheese
• ½ teaspoon dried oregano
• 32 wontons
• 1 cup water

Directions:
1. Preheat the toaster oven to 370°F.
2. In a medium bowl, mix together the refried beans and salsa.
3. In a second medium bowl, mix together the artichoke hearts, spinach, cream cheese, oregano, garlic powder, onion powder, and salt.
4. In a third medium bowl, mix together the pepperoni, mozzarella cheese, Parmesan cheese, cream cheese, and the remaining ½ teaspoon of oregano.
5. Get a towel lightly damp with water and ring it out. While working with the wontons, leave the unfilled wontons under the damp towel so they don't dry out.
6. Working with 8 wontons at a time, place 2 teaspoons of one of the fillings into the center of the wonton, rotating among the different fillings (one filling per wonton). Working one at a time, use a pastry brush, dip the pastry brush into the water, and brush the edges of the dough with the water. Fold the dough in half to form a triangle and set aside. Continue until 8 wontons are formed. Spray the wontons with cooking spray and cover with a dry towel. Repeat until all 32 wontons have been filled.
7. Place the wontons into the air fryer oven, leaving space between the wontons, and air-fry for 5 minutes. Turn over and check for brownness, and then air-fry for another 5 minutes.

Cheese Straws

Servings: 8
Cooking Time: 7 Minutes
Ingredients:
- For dusting All-purpose flour
- Two quarters of one thawed sheet (that is, a half of the sheet cut into two even pieces; wrap and refreeze the remainder) A 17.25-ounce box frozen puff pastry
- 1 Large egg(s)
- 2 tablespoons Water
- ¼ cup (about ¾ ounce) Finely grated Parmesan cheese
- up to 1 teaspoon Ground black pepper

Directions:
1. Preheat the toaster oven to 400°F.
2. Dust a clean, dry work surface with flour. Set one of the pieces of puff pastry on top, dust the pastry lightly with flour, and roll with a rolling pin to a 6-inch square.
3. Whisk the egg(s) and water in a small or medium bowl until uniform. Brush the pastry square(s) generously with this mixture. Sprinkle each square with 2 tablespoons grated cheese and up to ½ teaspoon ground black pepper.
4. Cut each square into 4 even strips. Grasp each end of 1 strip with clean, dry hands; twist it into a cheese straw. Place the twisted straws on a baking sheet.
5. Lay as many straws as will fit in the air-fryer oven—as a general rule, 4 of them in a small machine, 5 in a medium model, or 6 in a large. There should be space for air to

circulate around the straws. Set the baking sheet with any remaining straws in the fridge.
6. Air-fry undisturbed for 7 minutes, or until puffed and crisp. Use tongs to transfer the cheese straws to a wire rack, then make subsequent batches in the same way (keeping the baking sheet with the remaining straws in the fridge as each batch cooks). Serve warm.

Rumaki

Servings: 24
Cooking Time: 12 Minutes
Ingredients:
- 10 ounces raw chicken livers
- 1 can sliced water chestnuts, drained
- ¼ cup low-sodium teriyaki sauce
- 12 slices turkey bacon
- toothpicks

Directions:
1. Cut livers into 1½-inch pieces, trimming out tough veins as you slice.
2. Place livers, water chestnuts, and teriyaki sauce in small container with lid. If needed, add another tablespoon of teriyaki sauce to make sure livers are covered. Refrigerate for 1 hour.
3. When ready to cook, cut bacon slices in half crosswise.
4. Wrap 1 piece of liver and 1 slice of water chestnut in each bacon strip. Secure with toothpick.
5. When you have wrapped half of the livers, place them in the air fryer oven in a single layer.
6. Air-fry at 390°F for 12 minutes, until liver is done and bacon is crispy.
7. While first batch cooks, wrap the remaining livers. Repeat step 6 to cook your second batch.

Garlic Parmesan Kale Chips

Servings: 2
Cooking Time: 6 Minutes
Ingredients:
- 16 large kale leaves, washed and thick stems removed
- 1 tablespoon avocado oil
- ½ teaspoon garlic powder
- 1 teaspoon soy sauce or tamari
- ¼ cup grated Parmesan cheese

Directions:
1. Preheat the toaster oven to 370°F.
2. Make a stack of kale leaves and cut them into 4 pieces.
3. Place the kale pieces into a large bowl. Drizzle the avocado oil onto the kale and rub to coat. Add the garlic powder, soy sauce or tamari, and cheese, tossing to coat.
4. Pour the chips into the air fryer oven and air-fry for 6 minutes, checking for crispness every minute. When done cooking, pour the kale chips onto paper towels and cool at least 5 minutes before serving.

Veggie Chips

Servings:
Cooking Time: Minutes
Ingredients:
- sweet potato
- large parsnip
- large carrot
- turnip
- large beet
- vegetable or canola oil, in a spray bottle
- salt

Directions:
1. You can do a medley of vegetable chips, or just select from the vegetables listed. Whatever you choose to do, scrub the vegetables well and then slice them paper-thin using a mandolin (about -1/16 inch thick).
2. Preheat the toaster oven to 400°F.
3. Air-fry the chips in batches, one type of vegetable at a time. Spray the chips lightly with oil and transfer them to the air fryer oven. The key is to NOT over-load the air fryer oven. You can overlap the chips a little, but don't pile them on top of each other. Doing so will make it much harder to get evenly browned and crispy chips. Air-fry at 400°F for the time indicated below.
4. Sweet Potato – 8 to 9 minutes
5. Parsnips – 5 minutes
6. Carrot – 7 minutes
7. Turnips – 8 minutes
8. Beets – 9 minutes
9. Season the chips with salt during the last couple of minutes of air-frying. Check the chips as they cook until they are done to your liking. Some will start to brown sooner than others.
10. You can enjoy the chips warm out of the air fryer oven or cool them to room temperature for crispier chips.

Maple-glazed Acorn Squash

Servings: 2
Cooking Time: 30 Minutes
Ingredients:
- 1 acorn squash (1½ pounds), halved pole to pole, seeded, and cut into 8 wedges
- 1 tablespoon vegetable oil
- 1 teaspoon sugar
- ¼ teaspoon plus pinch table salt, divided
- ¼ teaspoon pepper
- 2 tablespoons maple syrup
- 2 tablespoons unsalted butter
- Pinch cayenne pepper
- 1 teaspoon fresh thyme leaves (optional)

Directions:
1. Adjust toaster oven rack to middle position and preheat the toaster oven to 450 degrees. Toss squash, oil, sugar, ¼ teaspoon salt, and pepper together on small rimmed baking sheet, then arrange cut side down in single layer. Roast until bottoms of squash wedges are deep golden brown, 15 to 20 minutes.
2. Meanwhile, microwave maple syrup, butter, cayenne, and remaining pinch salt in bowl, stirring occasionally, until butter is melted and mixture is slightly thickened, about 90 seconds; cover to keep warm.
3. Remove sheet from oven, and, using spatula, carefully flip squash. Brush with half of glaze and continue to roast until squash is tender and deep golden, 5 to 8 minutes. Carefully flip squash and brush with remaining glaze. Transfer squash to serving platter and sprinkle with thyme, if using. Serve.

Harissa Roasted Carrots

Servings: 3
Cooking Time: 25 Minutes
Ingredients:
- 1 tablespoon harissa
- 1 tablespoon honey
- 1 tablespoon olive oil
- ¼ teaspoon salt
- 5 large carrots, sliced in half lengthwise
- Chopped parsley, for garnish
- Pomegranate seeds, for garnish
- Chopped toasted walnuts, for garnish

Directions:
1. Combine the harissa, honey, olive oil, and salt in a bowl and whisk together.
2. Select the Preheat function on the Cosori Smart Air Fryer Toaster Oven and press Start/Pause.
3. Line the food tray with foil and place carrots on the tray. Pour the harissa mixture over the carrots and toss to evenly coat.
4. Insert the food tray at mid position in the preheated oven.
5. Select the Bake function, adjust time to 25 minutes, and press Start/Pause.
6. Remove when carrots are golden and tender.
7. Place carrots on a serving platter and garnish with chopped parsley, pomegranate seeds, and walnuts.

Crispy Chili Kale Chips

Servings: 4
Cooking Time: 10 Minutes
Ingredients:
- 2 cups kale, stemmed and torn into 2-inch pieces
- 1 tablespoon extra-virgin olive oil
- ½ teaspoon chipotle chili powder
- Sea salt, for seasoning

Directions:
1. Preheat the toaster oven to 350°F on AIR FRY for 5 minutes.
2. Dry the kale with paper towels. Transfer the kale to a medium bowl and add the olive oil and chili powder. Toss the kale using your hands to evenly coat the leaves with the oil.
3. Place the air-fryer basket in the baking sheet and spread the kale in a single layer in the basket. You might have to cook two batches.
4. Air fry in position 2 for 5 minutes, until the leaves are crispy.
5. Transfer the kale chips to a large bowl and repeat with the remaining kale. Season the chips with salt and serve immediately.

Spanakopita Spinach, Feta And Pine Nut Phyllo Bites

Servings: 8
Cooking Time: 10 Minutes
Ingredients:
- ½ (10-ounce) package frozen spinach, thawed and squeezed dry (about 1 cup)
- ¾ cup crumbled feta cheese
- ¼ cup grated Parmesan cheese
- ¼ cup pine nuts, toasted
- ⅛ teaspoon ground nutmeg
- 1 egg, lightly beaten
- ½ teaspoon salt
- freshly ground black pepper
- 6 sheets phyllo dough
- ½ cup butter, melted

Directions:
1. Combine the spinach, cheeses, pine nuts, nutmeg and egg in a bowl. Season with salt and freshly ground black pepper.
2. While building the phyllo triangles, always keep the dough sheets you are not working with covered with plastic wrap and a damp clean kitchen towel. Remove one sheet of the phyllo and place it on a flat surface. Brush the phyllo sheet with melted butter and then layer another sheet of phyllo on top. Brush the second sheet of phyllo with butter. Cut the layered phyllo sheets into 6 strips, about 2½- to 3-inches wide.
3. Place a heaping tablespoon of the spinach filling at the end of each strip of dough. Fold the bottom right corner of the strip over the filling towards the left edge of the strip to make a triangle. Continue to fold the phyllo dough around the spinach as you would fold a flag, making triangle after triangle. Brush the outside of the phyllo triangle with more melted butter and set it aside until you've finished the 6 strips of dough, making 6 triangles.
4. Preheat the toaster oven to 350°F.
5. Transfer the first six phyllo triangles to the air fryer oven and air-fry for 5 minutes. Turn the triangles over and air-fry for another 5 minutes.
6. While the first batch of triangles is air-frying, build another set of triangles and air-fry in the same manner. You should do three batches total. These can be warmed in the air fryer oven for a minute or two just before serving if you like.

Oven-baked Farro With Vegetables

Servings: 6
Cooking Time: 55 Minutes
Ingredients:
- Nonstick cooking spray
- 2 tablespoons olive oil
- ½ medium red onion, chopped
- ½ medium red bell pepper, chopped
- 1 carrot, chopped
- 2 cloves garlic, minced
- Kosher salt and freshly ground black pepper
- ½ cup pearled farro, rinsed and drained
- 1 (14.5-ounce) can diced tomatoes, with liquid
- 2 teaspoons white wine vinegar
- 2 tablespoons minced fresh basil or flat-leaf (Italian) parsley

Directions:
1. Preheat the toaster oven to 375°F. Spray a 2-quart casserole with nonstick cooking spray.
2. Heat the olive oil in a large skillet over medium-high heat. Add the onion, bell pepper, and carrot and cook, stirring frequently, for 3 to 5 minutes, or until the vegetables are tender. Stir in the garlic and cook for 30 seconds. Season with salt and pepper.
3. Stir in the farro and cook, stirring frequently, until the farro is toasted and golden brown. Stir in the tomatoes, vinegar, and 2 tablespoons water. Spoon into the prepared casserole dish. Cover and bake for 45 to 55 minutes or until the farro is tender.
4. Sprinkle with the basil just before serving.

Brazilian Cheese Bread (pão De Queijo)

Servings: 8
Cooking Time: 18 Minutes
Ingredients:

- 1 large egg, room temperature
- ⅓ cup olive oil
- ⅔ cups whole milk 1½ cups tapioca flour
- ½ cup feta cheese
- ¼ cup Parmesan cheese
- 1 teaspoon kosher salt
- ¼ teaspoon garlic powder
- Cooking spray

Directions:

1. Blend the egg, olive oil, milk, tapioca flour, feta, Parmesan, salt, and garlic powder in a stand mixer until smooth.
2. Spray the mini muffin pan with cooking spray.
3. Pour the batter into the muffin cups so they are ¾ full.
4. .Preheat the toaster oven to 380°F.
5. Place the muffin pan on the wire rack, then insert rack at mid position in the preheated oven.
6. Select the Bake function, adjust time to 18 minutes, and press Start/Pause.
7. Remove when done, then carefully pop the bread from the mini muffin tin and serve.

Simple Holiday Stuffing

Servings: 4
Cooking Time: 120 Minutes
Ingredients:

- 12 ounces hearty white sandwich bread, cut into ½-inch pieces (8 cups)
- 1 onion, chopped fine
- 1 celery rib, chopped fine
- 1 tablespoon unsalted butter, plus 5 tablespoons, melted
- 1 tablespoon minced fresh thyme or 1 teaspoon dried
- 2 teaspoons minced fresh sage or ½ teaspoon dried
- ¾ teaspoon table salt
- ¼ teaspoon pepper
- 1¼ cups chicken broth

Directions:

1. Adjust toaster oven rack to middle position and preheat the toaster oven to 300 degrees. Spread bread into even layer on small rimmed baking sheet and bake until light golden brown, 35 to 45 minutes, tossing halfway through baking. Let bread cool completely on sheet.
2. Increase oven temperature to 375 degrees. Microwave onion, celery, 1 tablespoon butter, thyme, sage, salt, and pepper in covered large bowl, stirring occasionally, until vegetables are softened, 2 to 4 minutes.
3. Stir in broth, then add bread and toss to combine. Let mixture sit for 10 minutes, then toss mixture again until broth is fully absorbed. Transfer bread mixture to 8-inch square baking dish or pan and distribute evenly but do not pack down. (Stuffing can be covered and refrigerated for up to 24 hours; increase covered baking time to 15 minutes.)
4. Drizzle melted butter evenly over top of stuffing. Cover dish tightly with aluminum foil and bake for 10 minutes. Uncover and continue to bake until top is golden brown and crisp, 15 to 25 minutes. Transfer dish to wire rack and let cool for 10 minutes. Serve.

Fish And Seafood

Fish And Seafood

Catfish Kebabs

Servings: 4
Cooking Time: 20 Minutes
Ingredients:
- Marinade:
- 3 tablespoons lemon juice
- 3 tablespoons tomato juice
- 2 garlic cloves, minced
- 2 tablespoons olive oil
- 1 teaspoon soy sauce
- 4 5-ounce catfish fillets
- 4 9-inch metal skewers
- 2 plum tomatoes, quartered
- 1 onion, cut into 1 × 1-inch pieces

Directions:
1. Combine the marinade ingredients in a small bowl. Set aside.
2. Cut the fillets into 2 by 3-inch strips and place in a shallow glass or ceramic dish. Add the marinade and refrigerate, covered, for at least 20 minutes. Remove the strips from the marinade, roll, and skewer, alternating the rolled strips with the tomatoes and onion.
3. Brush the kebabs with marinade, reserving the remaining marinade for brushing again later. Place the skewers on a broiling rack with a pan underneath.
4. Broil for 10 minutes, then remove the pan from the oven and carefully turn the skewers. Brush the kebabs with the marinade and broil again for 10 minutes, or until browned.

Crispy Calamari

Servings: 4
Cooking Time: 30 Minutes
Ingredients:
- Oil spray (hand-pumped)
- ¾ cup buttermilk
- 1 large egg
- 1 cup panko bread crumbs
- ¾ cup all-purpose flour
- ½ teaspoon sea salt or Old Bay seasoning
- 1 pound frozen squid rings, thawed and drained well or fresh
- 1 lemon, cut into wedges

Directions:
1. Preheat the toaster oven to 400°F on AIR FRY for 5 minutes.
2. Place the air-fryer basket in the baking tray and generously spray it with the oil.
3. In a medium bowl, whisk the buttermilk and egg.

4. In another medium bowl, stir the bread crumbs, flour, and salt until well blended.
5. Dredge the squid in the buttermilk mixture and then dredge it in the bread crumb mixture.
6. Place the breaded calamari in the basket in a single layer and lightly spray it with the oil. You will have to do several batches.
7. In position 2, air fry for 10 minutes until crispy and golden brown. Cover the cooked calamari with foil to keep it warm while you cook the remaining batches.
8. Repeat with the remaining calamari rings.
9. Serve with lemon wedges.

Crab Cakes

Servings: 4
Cooking Time: 9 Minutes
Ingredients:
- 1 pound lump crab meat, checked for shells
- ⅓ cup breadcrumbs
- ¼ cup finely chopped onions
- ¼ cup finely chopped red bell peppers
- ¼ cup finely chopped parsley
- ¼ teaspoon sea salt
- 2 eggs, whisked
- ¾ cup mayonnaise, divided
- ¼ cup sour cream
- 1 lemon, divided
- ¼ cup sweet pickle relish
- 1 tablespoon prepared mustard

Directions:
1. In a large bowl, mix together the crab meat, breadcrumbs, onions, bell peppers, parsley, sea salt, eggs, and ¼ cup of the mayonnaise.
2. Preheat the toaster oven to 380°F.
3. Form 8 patties with the crab cake mixture. Line the air fryer oven with parchment paper and place the crab cakes on the parchment paper. Spray with cooking spray. Air-fry for 4 minutes, turn over the crab cakes, spray with cooking spray, and air-fry for an additional 3 to 5 minutes, or until golden brown and the edges are crispy. Cook in batches as needed.
4. Meanwhile, make the sauce. In a small bowl, mix together the remaining ½ cup of mayonnaise, the sour cream, the juice from ½ of the lemon, the pickle relish, and the mustard.
5. Place the cooked crab cakes on a serving platter and serve with the remaining ½ lemon cut into wedges and the dipping sauce.

Crispy Smelts

Servings: 3
Cooking Time: 20 Minutes
Ingredients:
- 1 pound Cleaned smelts
- 3 tablespoons Tapioca flour
- Vegetable oil spray
- To taste Coarse sea salt or kosher salt

Directions:
1. Preheat the toaster oven to 400°F.
2. Toss the smelts and tapioca flour in a large bowl until the little fish are evenly coated.
3. Lay the smelts out on a large cutting board. Lightly coat both sides of each fish with vegetable oil spray.
4. When the machine is at temperature, set the smelts close together in the air fryer oven, with a few even overlapping on top. Air-fry undisturbed for 20 minutes, until lightly browned and crisp.
5. Remove from the machine and turn out the fish onto a wire rack. The smelts will most likely come out as one large block, or maybe in a couple of large pieces. Cool for a minute or two, then sprinkle the smelts with salt and break the block(s) into much smaller sections or individual fish to serve.

Quick Shrimp Scampi

Servings: 2
Cooking Time: 5 Minutes
Ingredients:
- 16 to 20 raw large shrimp, peeled, deveined and tails removed
- ½ cup white wine
- freshly ground black pepper
- ¼ cup + 1 tablespoon butter, divided
- 1 clove garlic, sliced
- 1 teaspoon olive oil
- salt, to taste
- juice of ½ lemon, to taste
- ¼ cup chopped fresh parsley

Directions:
1. Start by marinating the shrimp in the white wine and freshly ground black pepper for at least 30 minutes, or as long as 2 hours in the refrigerator.
2. Preheat the toaster oven to 400°F.
3. Melt ¼ cup of butter in a small saucepan on the stovetop. Add the garlic and let the butter simmer, but be sure to not let it burn.
4. Pour the shrimp and marinade into the air fryer oven, letting the marinade drain through to the bottom drawer. Drizzle the olive oil on the shrimp and season well with salt. Air-fry at 400°F for 3 minutes. Turn the shrimp over and pour the garlic butter over the shrimp. Air-fry for another 2 minutes.

5. Remove the shrimp from the air fryer oven and transfer them to a bowl. Squeeze lemon juice over all the shrimp and toss with the chopped parsley and remaining tablespoon of butter. Season to taste with salt and serve immediately.

Rolled Asparagus Flounder

Servings: 4
Cooking Time: 30 Minutes
Ingredients:
- 1 dozen asparagus stalks, tough stem part cut off
- 4 6-ounce flounder fillets
- 4 tablespoons chopped scallions
- 4 tablespoons shredded carrots
- 4 tablespoons finely chopped
- Almonds
- 1 teaspoon dried dill weed
- Salt and freshly ground black pepper
- 1 lemon, cut into wedges

Directions:
1. Preheat the toaster oven to 400° F.
2. Place 3 asparagus stalks lengthwise on a flounder fillet. Add 1 tablespoon scallions, 1 tablespoon carrots, 1 tablespoon almonds, and a sprinkling of dill. Season to taste with salt and pepper and roll the fillet together so that the long edges overlap. Secure the edges with toothpicks or tie with cotton string. Carefully place the rolled fillet in an oiled or nonstick 8½ × 8½ × 2-inch square baking (cake) pan. Repeat the process for the remaining ingredients. Cover the pan with aluminum foil.
3. BAKE, covered, for 20 minutes, or until the asparagus is tender. Remove the cover.
4. BROIL, uncovered, for 10 minutes, or until the fish is lightly browned. Remove and discard the toothpicks or string. Serve the rolled filets with lemon wedges.

Better Fish Sticks

Servings: 3
Cooking Time: 8 Minutes
Ingredients:
- ¾ cup Seasoned Italian-style dried bread crumbs (gluten-free, if a concern)
- 3 tablespoons (about ½ ounce) Finely grated Parmesan cheese
- 10 ounces Skinless cod fillets, cut lengthwise into 1-inch-wide pieces
- 3 tablespoons Regular or low-fat mayonnaise (not fat-free; gluten-free, if a concern)
- Vegetable oil spray

Directions:
1. Preheat the toaster oven to 400°F.
2. Mix the bread crumbs and grated Parmesan in a shallow soup bowl or a small pie plate.
3. Smear the fish fillet sticks completely with the mayon-

naise, then dip them one by one in the bread-crumb mixture, turning and pressing gently to make an even and thorough coating. Coat each stick on all sides with vegetable oil spray.

4. Set the fish sticks in the air fryer oven with at least ¼ inch between them. Air-fry undisturbed for 8 minutes, or until golden brown and crisp.

5. Use a nonstick-safe spatula to gently transfer them from the air fryer oven to a wire rack. Cool for only a minute or two before serving.

Lightened-up Breaded Fish Filets

Servings: 4
Cooking Time: 10 Minutes
Ingredients:
- ½ cup all-purpose flour
- ½ teaspoon cayenne pepper
- 1 teaspoon garlic powder
- ½ teaspoon black pepper
- ¼ teaspoon salt
- 2 eggs, whisked
- 1½ cups panko breadcrumbs
- 1 pound boneless white fish filets
- 1 cup tartar sauce
- 1 lemon, sliced into wedges

Directions:
1. In a medium bowl, mix the flour, cayenne pepper, garlic powder, pepper, and salt.
2. In a shallow dish, place the eggs.
3. In a third dish, place the breadcrumbs.
4. Cover the fish in the flour, dip them in the egg, and coat them with panko. Repeat until all fish are covered in the breading.
5. Liberally spray the metal trivet that fits inside the air fryer oven with olive oil mist. Place the fish onto the trivet, leaving space between the filets to flip. Air-fry for 5 minutes, flip the fish, and cook another 5 minutes. Repeat until all the fish is cooked.
6. Serve warm with tartar sauce and lemon wedges.

Fish And "chips"

Servings: 2
Cooking Time: 10 Minutes
Ingredients:
- ½ cup flour
- ½ teaspoon paprika
- ¼ teaspoon ground white pepper (or freshly ground black pepper)
- 1 egg
- ¼ cup mayonnaise
- 2 cups salt & vinegar kettle cooked potato chips, coarsely crushed
- 12 ounces cod

- tartar sauce
- lemon wedges

Directions:
1. Set up a dredging station. Combine the flour, paprika and pepper in a shallow dish. Combine the egg and mayonnaise in a second shallow dish. Place the crushed potato chips in a third shallow dish.
2. Cut the cod into 6 pieces. Dredge each piece of fish in the flour, then dip it into the egg mixture and then place it into the crushed potato chips. Make sure all sides of the fish are covered and pat the chips gently onto the fish so they stick well.
3. Preheat the toaster oven to 370°F.
4. Place the coated fish fillets into the air fry oven. (It is ok if a couple of pieces slightly overlap or rest on top of other fillets in order to fit everything in the air fryer oven.)
5. Air-fry for 10 minutes, gently turning the fish over halfway through the cooking time.
6. Transfer the fish to a platter and serve with tartar sauce and lemon wedges.

Oven-poached Salmon

Servings: 2
Cooking Time: 20 Minutes
Ingredients:
- Poaching liquid:
- 1 cup dry white wine
- 2 bay leaves
- 1 tablespoon mustard seed
- Salt and freshly ground black pepper to taste
- 2 6-ounce salmon steaks
- 2 tablespoons fresh watercress, rinsed, drained, and chopped (for serving hot)
- 1 lemon, cut into small wedges (for serving hot)
- Cucumber Sauce (recipe follows)

Directions:
1. Preheat the toaster oven to 350° F.
2. Combine the poaching liquid ingredients with 1 cup water in a small bowl and set aside.
3. Place the salmon steaks in an oiled or nonstick 8½ × 8½ × 2-inch square baking (cake) pan and pour enough poaching liquid over the steaks to barely cover them. Adjust the seasonings to taste.
4. BAKE, uncovered, for 20 minutes, or until the fish feels springy to the touch. Remove the bay leaves and serve the fish hot with watercress and lemon or cold with Cucumber Sauce.

Crab-stuffed Peppers

Servings: 4
Cooking Time: 45 Minutes
Ingredients:
- Filling:
- 1½ cups fresh crabmeat, chopped, or 2 6-ounce cans lump crabmeat, drained
- 4 plum tomatoes, chopped
- 2 4-ounce cans sliced mushrooms, drained well
- 4 tablespoons pitted and sliced black olives
- 2 tablespoons olive oil
- 2 garlic cloves, minced
- ½ teaspoon ground cumin
- Salt and freshly ground black pepper to taste
- 4 large bell peppers, tops cut off, seeds and membrane removed
- ½ cup shredded low-fat mozzarella cheese

Dircetions:
1. Preheat the toaster oven to 375° F.
2. Combine the filling ingredients in a bowl and adjust the seasonings. Spoon the mixture to generously fill each pepper. Place the peppers upright in an 8½ × 8½ × 2-inch oiled or nonstick square (cake) pan.
3. BAKE for 40 minutes, or until the peppers are tender. Remove from the oven and sprinkle the cheese in equal portions on top of the peppers.
4. BROIL 5 minutes, or until the cheese is melted.

Cajun Flounder Fillets

Servings: 2
Cooking Time: 5 Minutes
Ingredients:
- 2 4-ounce skinless flounder fillet(s)
- 2 teaspoons Peanut oil
- 1 teaspoon Purchased or homemade Cajun dried seasoning blend

Directions:
1. Preheat the toaster oven to 400°F.
2. Oil the fillet(s) by drizzling on the peanut oil, then gently rubbing in the oil with your clean, dry fingers. Sprinkle the seasoning blend evenly over both sides of the fillet(s).
3. When the machine is at temperature, set the fillet(s) in the air fryer oven. If working with more than one fillet, they should not touch, although they may be quite close together, depending on the air fryer oven's size. Air-fry undisturbed for 5 minutes, or until lightly browned and cooked through.
4. Use a nonstick-safe spatula to transfer the fillets to a serving platter or plate(s). Serve at once.

Best-dressed Trout

Servings: 2
Cooking Time: 25 Minutes
Ingredients:
- 2 dressed trout
- 1 egg, beaten
- 2 tablespoons finely ground almonds
- 2 tablespoons unbleached flour
- 1 teaspoon paprika or smoked paprika
- Pinch of salt (optional)
- 4 lemon slices, approximately ¼ inch thick
- 1 teaspoon lemon juice

Directions:
1. Preheat the toaster oven to 400° F.
2. Brush the trout (both sides) with the beaten egg. Blend the almonds, flour, paprika, and salt in a bowl and sprinkle both sides of the trout. Insert 2 lemon slices in each trout cavity and place the trout in an oiled or nonstick 8½ × 8½ × 2-inch square baking (cake) pan.
3. BAKE for 20 minutes, or until the meat is white and firm. Remove from the oven and turn the trout carefully with a spatula.
4. BROIL for 5 minutes, or until the trout is lightly browned.

Shrimp, Chorizo And Fingerling Potatoes

Servings: 4
Cooking Time: 16 Minutes
Ingredients:
- ½ red onion, chopped into 1-inch chunks
- 8 fingerling potatoes, sliced into 1-inch slices or halved lengthwise
- 1 teaspoon olive oil
- salt and freshly ground black pepper
- 8 ounces raw chorizo sausage, sliced into 1-inch chunks
- 16 raw large shrimp, peeled, deveined and tails removed
- 1 lime
- ¼ cup chopped fresh cilantro
- chopped orange zest (optional)

Directions:
1. Preheat the toaster oven to 380°F.
2. Combine the red onion and potato chunks in a bowl and toss with the olive oil, salt and freshly ground black pepper.
3. Transfer the vegetables to the air fryer oven and air-fry for 6 minutes.
4. Add the chorizo chunks and continue to air-fry for another 5 minutes.
5. Add the shrimp, season with salt and continue to air-fry for another 5 minutes.
6. Transfer the tossed shrimp, chorizo and potato to a bowl and squeeze some lime juice over the top to taste. Toss in

the fresh cilantro, orange zest and a drizzle of olive oil, and season again to taste.

7. Serve with a fresh green salad.

Sweet Chili Shrimp

Servings: 4
Cooking Time: 6 Minutes
Ingredients:
- 1 pound jumbo shrimp, peeled and deveined
- ¼ cup sweet chili sauce
- 1 lime, zested and juiced
- 1 tablespoon soy sauce
- 1 tablespoon honey
- 1 tablespoon olive oil
- 1 large garlic clove, minced
- ½ teaspoon salt
- ¼ teaspoon pepper
- 1 green onion, thinly sliced, for garnish

Directions:
1. Place the shrimp in a large bowl. Whisk all the remaining ingredients except the green onion in a separate bowl.
2. Pour sauce over the shrimp and toss to coat.
3. Preheat the toaster Oven to 430°F.
4. Line the food tray with foil, place shrimp on the tray, then insert at top position in the preheated oven.
5. Select the Air Fry function, adjust time to 6 minutes, and press Start/Pause.
6. Remove shrimp and garnish with sliced green onions.

Baked Tomato Pesto Bluefish

Servings: 2
Cooking Time: 23 Minutes
Ingredients:
- 2 plum tomatoes
- 2 tablespoons tomato paste
- ¼ cup fresh basil leaves
- 1 tablespoon olive oil
- 2 garlic cloves
- 2 tablespoons pine nuts
- ¼ cup grated Parmesan cheese
- 1 teaspoon dried oregano
- Salt to taste
- 2 6-ounce bluefish fillets

Directions:
1. Preheat the toaster oven to 400° F.
2. Process the pesto ingredients in a blender or food processor until smooth.
3. Place the bluefish fillets in an oiled or nonstick 8½ × 8½ × 2-inch square baking (cake) pan.
4. BAKE, covered, for 15 minutes, or until the fish flakes with a fork. Remove from the oven, uncover, and spread the pesto mixture on both sides of the fillets.
5. BROIL, uncovered, for 8 minutes, or until the pesto is

lightly browned.

Popcorn Crawfish

Servings: 4
Cooking Time: 18 Minutes
Ingredients:
- ½ cup flour, plus 2 tablespoons
- ½ teaspoon garlic powder
- 1½ teaspoons Old Bay Seasoning
- ½ teaspoon onion powder
- ½ cup beer, plus 2 tablespoons
- 12-ounce package frozen crawfish tail meat, thawed and drained
- oil for misting or cooking spray
- Coating
- 1½ cups panko crumbs
- 1 teaspoon Old Bay Seasoning
- ½ teaspoon ground black pepper

Directions:
1. In a large bowl, mix together the flour, garlic powder, Old Bay Seasoning, and onion powder. Stir in beer to blend.
2. Add crawfish meat to batter and stir to coat.
3. Combine the coating ingredients in food processor and pulse to finely crush the crumbs. Transfer crumbs to shallow dish.
4. Preheat the toaster oven to 390°F.
5. Pour the crawfish and batter into a colander to drain. Stir with a spoon to drain excess batter.
6. Working with a handful of crawfish at a time, roll in crumbs and place on a cookie sheet. It's okay if some of the smaller pieces of crawfish meat stick together.
7. Spray breaded crawfish with oil or cooking spray and place all at once into air fryer oven.
8. Air-fry at 390°F for 5 minutes. Stir and mist again with olive oil or spray. Cook 5 more minutes, stir again, and mist lightly again. Continue cooking 5 more minutes, until browned and crispy.

Maple Balsamic Glazed Salmon

Servings: 4
Cooking Time: 10 Minutes
Ingredients:
- 4 (6-ounce) fillets of salmon
- salt and freshly ground black pepper
- vegetable oil
- ¼ cup pure maple syrup
- 3 tablespoons balsamic vinegar
- 1 teaspoon Dijon mustard

Directions:
1. Preheat the toaster oven to 400°F.
2. Season the salmon well with salt and freshly ground black pepper. Spray or brush the bottom of the air fryer oven with vegetable oil and place the salmon fillets inside.

Air-fry the salmon for 5 minutes.

3. While the salmon is air-frying, combine the maple syrup, balsamic vinegar and Dijon mustard in a small saucepan over medium heat and stir to blend well. Let the mixture simmer while the fish is cooking. It should start to thicken slightly, but keep your eye on it so it doesn't burn.

4. Brush the glaze on the salmon fillets and air-fry for an additional 5 minutes. The salmon should feel firm to the touch when finished and the glaze should be nicely browned on top. Brush a little more glaze on top before removing and serving with rice and vegetables, or a nice green salad.

Romaine Wraps With Shrimp Filling

Servings: 4
Cooking Time: 8 Minutes
Ingredients:
- Filling:
- 1 6-ounce can tiny shrimp, drained, or 1 cup fresh shrimp, peeled, cooked, and chopped
- ¾ cup canned chickpeas, mashed into 1 tablespoon olive oil
- 2 tablespoons chopped fresh parsley
- 2 tablespoons grated carrot
- 2 tablespoons chopped bell pepper
- 2 tablespoons minced onion
- 2 tablespoons lemon juice
- 1 teaspoon soy sauce
- Freshly ground black pepper to taste
- 4 large romaine lettuce leaves Olive oil
- 3 tablespoons lemon juice
- 1 teaspoon paprika
Directions:
1. Combine the filling ingredients in a bowl, adjusting the seasonings to taste. Spoon equal portions of the filling into the centers of the romaine leaves. Fold the leaves in half, pressing the filling together, overlap the leaf edges, and skewer with toothpicks to fasten. Carefully place the leaves in an oiled or nonstick 8½ × 8½ × 2-inch square baking (cake) pan. Lightly spray or brush the lettuce rolls with olive oil.

2. BROIL for 8 minutes, or until the filling is cooked and the leaves are lightly browned. Remove from the oven, remove the toothpicks, and drizzle with the lemon juice and sprinkle with paprika.

Shrimp With Jalapeño Dip

Servings: 4
Cooking Time: 10 Minutes
Ingredients:
- Seasonings:
- 1 teaspoon ground cumin
- 1 tablespoon minced garlic
- 1 teaspoon paprika
- 1 teaspoon chili powder
- Pinch of cayenne
- Salt to taste
- 1½ pounds large shrimp, peeled and deveined
Directions:
1. Combine the seasonings in a plastic bag, add the shrimp, and shake well to coat. Transfer the shrimp to an oiled or nonstick 8½ × 8½ × 2-inch square baking (cake) pan.

2. BROIL for 5 minutes. Remove the pan from the oven and turn the shrimp with tongs. Broil 5 minutes again, or until the shrimp are cooked (they should be firm but not rubbery.) Serve with Jalapeño Dip.

Blackened Red Snapper

Servings: 4
Cooking Time: 8 Minutes
Ingredients:
- 1½ teaspoons black pepper
- ¼ teaspoon thyme
- ¼ teaspoon garlic powder
- ⅛ teaspoon cayenne pepper
- 1 teaspoon olive oil
- 4 4-ounce red snapper fillet portions, skin on
- 4 thin slices lemon
- cooking spray
Directions:
1. Mix the spices and oil together to make a paste. Rub into both sides of the fish.

2. Spray air fryer oven with nonstick cooking spray and lay snapper steaks in air fryer oven, skin-side down.

3. Place a lemon slice on each piece of fish.

4. Air-fry at 390°F for 8 minutes. The fish will not flake when done, but it should be white through the center.

Light Trout Amandine

Servings: 4
Cooking Time: 15 Minutes
Ingredients:
- 1 tablespoon margarine
- ½ cup sliced almonds
- 1 tablespoon lemon juice
- 1 teaspoon Worcestershire sauce
- Salt and freshly ground black pepper
- 4 6-ounce trout fillets
- 2 tablespoons chopped fresh parsley
Directions:
1. Combine the margarine and almonds in an oiled or nonstick 8½ × 8½ × 2-inch square baking (cake) pan.

2. BROIL for 5 minutes, or until the margarine is melted. Remove the pan from the oven and add the lemon juice and Worcestershire sauce. Season to taste with salt and pepper, and stir again to blend well. Add the trout fillets and spoon the mixture over them to coat well.

3. BROIL for 10 minutes, or until the almonds and fillets are lightly browned. Garnish with the chopped parsley before serving.

Horseradish Crusted Salmon

Servings: 2
Cooking Time: 14 Minutes
Ingredients:
- 2 (5-ounce) salmon fillets
- salt and freshly ground black pepper
- 2 teaspoons Dijon mustard
- ½ cup panko breadcrumbs
- 2 tablespoons prepared horseradish
- ½ teaspoon finely chopped lemon zest
- 1 tablespoon olive oil
- 1 tablespoon chopped fresh parsley

Directions:
1. Preheat the toaster oven to 360°F.
2. Season the salmon with salt and freshly ground black pepper. Then spread the Dijon mustard on the salmon, coating the entire surface.
3. Combine the breadcrumbs, horseradish, lemon zest and olive oil in a small bowl. Spread the mixture over the top of the salmon and press down lightly with your hands, adhering it to the salmon using the mustard as "glue".
4. Transfer the salmon to the air fryer oven and air-fry at 360°F for 14 minutes (depending on how thick your fillet is) or until the fish feels firm to the touch. Sprinkle with the parsley.

Ginger Miso Calamari

Servings: 4
Cooking Time: 10 Minutes
Ingredients:
- 15 ounces calamari, cleaned
- Sauce:
- 2 tablespoons dry white wine
- 2 tablespoons white miso
- 1 tablespoon balsamic vinegar
- 1 teaspoon honey
- 1 teaspoon toasted sesame oil
- 1 teaspoon olive oil
- 1 tablespoon grated fresh ginger
- Salt and white pepper to taste

Directions:
1. Slice the calamari bodies into ½-inch rings, leaving the tentacles uncut. Set aside.
2. Whisk together the sauce ingredients in a bowl. Transfer the mixture to a baking pan and add the calamari, mixing well to coat.
3. BROIL for 20 minutes, turning with tongs every 5 minutes, or until cooked but not rubbery. Serve with the sauce.

Spicy Fish Street Tacos With Sriracha Slaw

Servings: 2
Cooking Time: 5 Minutes
Ingredients:
- Sriracha Slaw:
- ½ cup mayonnaise
- 2 tablespoons rice vinegar
- 1 teaspoon sugar
- 2 tablespoons sriracha chili sauce
- 5 cups shredded green cabbage
- ¼ cup shredded carrots
- 2 scallions, chopped
- salt and freshly ground black pepper
- Tacos:
- ½ cup flour
- 1 teaspoon chili powder
- ½ teaspoon ground cumin
- 1 teaspoon salt
- freshly ground black pepper
- ½ teaspoon baking powder
- 1 egg, beaten
- ¼ cup milk
- 1 cup breadcrumbs
- 1 pound mahi-mahi or snapper fillets
- 1 tablespoon canola or vegetable oil
- 6 (6-inch) flour tortillas
- 1 lime, cut into wedges

Directions:
1. Start by making the sriracha slaw. Combine the mayonnaise, rice vinegar, sugar, and sriracha sauce in a large bowl. Mix well and add the green cabbage, carrots, and scallions. Toss until all the vegetables are coated with the dressing and season with salt and pepper. Refrigerate the slaw until you are ready to serve the tacos.
2. Combine the flour, chili powder, cumin, salt, pepper and baking powder in a bowl. Add the egg and milk and mix until the batter is smooth. Place the breadcrumbs in shallow dish.
3. Cut the fish fillets into 1-inch wide sticks, approximately 4-inches long. You should have about 12 fish sticks total. Dip the fish sticks into the batter, coating all sides. Let the excess batter drip off the fish and then roll them in the breadcrumbs, patting the crumbs onto all sides of the fish sticks. Set the coated fish on a plate or baking sheet until all the fish has been coated.
4. Preheat the toaster oven to 400°F.
5. Spray the coated fish sticks with oil on all sides. Spray or brush the inside of the air fryer oven with oil and transfer the fish to the air fryer oven. Place as many sticks as you can in one layer, leaving a little room around each stick. Place any remaining sticks on top, perpendicular to the first layer.

6. Air-fry the fish for 3 minutes. Turn the fish sticks over and air-fry for an additional 2 minutes.

7. While the fish is air-frying, warm the tortilla shells either in a 350°F oven wrapped in foil or in a skillet with a little oil over medium-high heat for a couple minutes. Fold the tortillas in half and keep them warm until the remaining tortillas and fish are ready.

8. To assemble the tacos, place two pieces of the fish in each tortilla shell and top with the sriracha slaw. Squeeze the lime wedge over top and dig in.

Fried Oysters

Servings: 12
Cooking Time: 8 Minutes

Ingredients:
- 1½ cups All-purpose flour
- 1½ cups Yellow cornmeal
- 1½ tablespoons Cajun dried seasoning blend
- 1¼ cups, plus more if needed Amber beer, pale ale, or IPA
- 12 Large shucked oysters, any liquid drained off
- Vegetable oil spray

Directions:
1. Preheat the toaster oven to 400°F.
2. Whisk ⅔ cup of the flour, ½ cup of the cornmeal, and the seasoning blend in a bowl until uniform. Set aside.
3. Whisk the remaining ⅓ cup flour and the remaining ½ cup cornmeal with the beer in a second bowl, adding more beer in dribs and drabs until the mixture is the consistency of pancake batter.
4. Using a fork, dip a shucked oyster in the beer batter, coating it thoroughly. Gently shake off any excess batter, then set the oyster in the dry mixture and turn gently to coat well and evenly. Set the coated oyster on a cutting board and continue dipping and coating the remainder of the oysters.
5. Coat the oysters with vegetable oil spray, then set them in the air fryer oven with as much air space between them as possible. Air-fry undisturbed for 8 minutes, or until lightly browned and crisp.
6. Use a nonstick-safe spatula to transfer the oysters to a wire rack. Cool for a couple of minutes before serving.

Crunchy Clam Strips

Servings: 3
Cooking Time: 8 Minutes

Ingredients:
- ½ pound Clam strips, drained
- 1 Large egg, well beaten
- ½ cup All-purpose flour
- ½ cup Yellow cornmeal
- 1½ teaspoons Table salt
- 1½ teaspoons Ground black pepper
- Up to ¾ teaspoon Cayenne
- Vegetable oil spray

Directions:
1. Preheat the toaster oven to 400°F.
2. Toss the clam strips and beaten egg in a bowl until the clams are well coated.
3. Mix the flour, cornmeal, salt, pepper, and cayenne in a large zip-closed plastic bag until well combined. Using a flatware fork or small kitchen tongs, lift the clam strips one by one out of the egg, letting any excess egg slip back into the rest. Put the strips in the bag with the flour mixture. Once all the strips are in the bag, seal it until the strips are well coated.
4. Use kitchen tongs to pick out the clam strips and lay them on a cutting board (leaving any extra flour mixture in the bag to be discarded). Coat the strips on both sides with vegetable oil spray.
5. When the machine is at temperature, spread the clam strips in the air fryer oven in one layer. They may touch in places, but try to leave as much air space as possible around them. Air-fry undisturbed for 8 minutes, or until brown and crunchy.
6. Gently dump the contents of the air fryer oven onto a serving platter. Cool for just a minute or two before serving hot.

Oven-crisped Fish Fillets With Salsa

Servings: 4
Cooking Time: 14 Minutes

Ingredients:
- Coating ingredients:
- 1 cup cornmeal
- 1 teaspoon garlic powder
- 1 teaspoon ground cumin
- 1 teaspoon paprika
- Salt to taste
- 4 6-ounce fish fillets, approximately
- ¼ to ½ inch thick
- 2 tablespoons vegetable oil

Directions:
1. Combine the coating ingredients in a small bowl, blending well. Transfer to a large plate, spreading evenly over the surface. Brush the fillets with vegetable oil and press both sides of each fillet into the coating.
2. BROIL an oiled or nonstick 8½ × 8½ × 2-inch square baking (cake) pan for 1 or 2 minutes to preheat. Remove the pan and place the fillets in the hot pan, laying them flat.
3. BROIL for 7 minutes, then remove the pan from the oven and carefully turn the fillets with a spatula. Broil for another 7 minutes, or until the fish flakes easily with a fork and the coating is crisped to your preference. Serve immediately.

Butternut Squash–wrapped Halibut Fillets

Servings: 3
Cooking Time: 11 Minutes
Ingredients:
- 15 Long spiralized peeled and seeded butternut squash strands
- 3 5- to 6-ounce skinless halibut fillets
- 3 tablespoons Butter, melted
- ¾ teaspoon Mild paprika
- ¾ teaspoon Table salt
- ¾ teaspoon Ground black pepper

Directions:
1. Preheat the toaster oven to 375°F .
2. Hold 5 long butternut squash strands together and wrap them around a fillet. Set it aside and wrap any remaining fillet(s).
3. Mix the melted butter, paprika, salt, and pepper in a small bowl. Brush this mixture over the squash-wrapped fillets on all sides.
4. When the machine is at temperature, set the fillets in the air fryer oven with as much air space between them as possible. Air-fry undisturbed for 10 minutes, or until the squash strands have browned but not burned. If the machine is at 360°F, you may need to add 1 minute to the cooking time. In any event, watch the fish carefully after the 8-minute mark.
5. Use a nonstick-safe spatula to gently transfer the fillets to a serving platter or plates. Cool for only a minute or so before serving.

Broiled Lemon Coconut Shrimp

Servings: 4
Cooking Time: 10 Minutes
Ingredients:
- Brushing mixture:
- 2 tablespoons lemon juice
- 4 tablespoons olive oil
- 1 tablespoon grated lemon zest
- Salt to taste
- 1 pound fresh shrimp, peeled, deveined, and butterflied
- ½ cup grated unsweetened coconut

Directions:
1. Combine the brushing mixture ingredients in a small bowl. Add the shrimp and toss to coat well. Set aside.
2. Place the coconut on a plate, spreading it out evenly.
3. Press each shrimp into the coconut, coating well on all sides. Place the shrimp in an 8½ × 8½ × 2-inch oiled or nonstick square (cake) pan.
4. BROIL the shrimp for 5 minutes, turn with tongs, and broil for 5 more minutes, or until browned lightly.

Sea Bass With Potato Scales And Caper Aïoli

Servings: 2
Cooking Time: 10 Minutes
Ingredients:
- 2 (6- to 8-ounce) fillets of sea bass
- salt and freshly ground black pepper
- ¼ cup mayonnaise
- 2 teaspoons finely chopped lemon zest
- 1 teaspoon chopped fresh thyme
- 2 fingerling potatoes, very thinly sliced into rounds
- olive oil
- ½ clove garlic, crushed into a paste
- 1 tablespoon capers, drained and rinsed
- 1 tablespoon olive oil
- 1 teaspoon lemon juice, to taste

Directions:
1. Preheat the toaster oven to 400°F.
2. Season the fish well with salt and freshly ground black pepper. Mix the mayonnaise, lemon zest and thyme together in a small bowl. Spread a thin layer of the mayonnaise mixture on both fillets. Start layering rows of potato slices onto the fish fillets to simulate the fish scales. The second row should overlap the first row slightly. Dabbing a little more mayonnaise along the upper edge of the row of potatoes where the next row overlaps will help the potato slices stick. Press the potatoes onto the fish to secure them well and season again with salt. Brush or spray the potato layer with olive oil.
3. Transfer the fish to the air fryer oven and air-fry for 8 to 10 minutes, depending on the thickness of your fillets. 1-inch of fish should take 10 minutes at 400°F.
4. While the fish is cooking, add the garlic, capers, olive oil and lemon juice to the remaining mayonnaise mixture to make the caper aïoli.
5. Serve the fish warm with a dollop of the aïoli on top or on the side.

Poultry

Poultry

Light And Lovely Loaf

Servings: 4
Cooking Time: 30 Minutes
Ingredients:
- 2 cups ground chicken or turkey breast
- 1 egg
- ½ cup grated carrot
- ½ cup grated celery
- 1 tablespoon finely chopped onion
- ½ teaspoon garlic powder
- Salt and freshly ground black pepper to taste

Directions:
1. Preheat the toaster oven to 400° F.
2. Blend all ingredients in a bowl, mixing well, and transfer to an oiled or nonstick regular-size 4½ × 8½ × 2¼-inch loaf pan
3. BAKE, uncovered, for 30 minutes, until lightly browned.

Sweet-and-sour Chicken

Servings: 6
Cooking Time: 10 Minutes
Ingredients:
- 1 cup pineapple juice
- 1 cup plus 3 tablespoons cornstarch, divided
- ¼ cup sugar
- ¼ cup ketchup
- ¼ cup apple cider vinegar
- 2 tablespoons soy sauce or tamari
- 1 teaspoon garlic powder, divided
- ¼ cup flour
- 1 tablespoon sesame seeds
- ½ teaspoon salt
- ¼ teaspoon ground black pepper
- 2 large eggs
- 2 pounds chicken breasts, cut into 1-inch cubes
- 1 red bell pepper, cut into 1-inch pieces
- 1 carrot, sliced into ¼-inch-thick rounds

Directions:
1. In a medium saucepan, whisk together the pineapple juice, 3 tablespoons of the cornstarch, the sugar, the ketchup, the apple cider vinegar, the soy sauce or tamari, and ½ teaspoon of the garlic powder. Cook over medium-low heat, whisking occasionally as the sauce thickens, about 6 minutes. Stir and set aside while preparing the chicken.
2. Preheat the toaster oven to 370°F.
3. In a medium bowl, place the remaining 1 cup of cornstarch, the flour, the sesame seeds, the salt, the remaining ½ teaspoon of garlic powder, and the pepper.

4. In a second medium bowl, whisk the eggs.
5. Working in batches, place the cubed chicken in the cornstarch mixture to lightly coat; then dip it into the egg mixture, and return it to the cornstarch mixture. Shake off the excess and place the coated chicken in the air fryer oven. Spray with cooking spray and air-fry for 5 minutes, and spray with more cooking spray. Cook an additional 3 to 5 minutes, or until completely cooked and golden brown.
6. On the last batch of chicken, add the bell pepper and carrot to the air fryer oven and cook with the chicken.
7. Place the cooked chicken and vegetables into a serving bowl and toss with the sweet-and-sour sauce to serve.

Roast Chicken

Servings: 6
Cooking Time: 90 Minutes
Ingredients:
- Nonstick cooking spray
- 1 whole (3 ½ -pound) chicken
- Grated zest and juice of 1 lemon
- 1 tablespoon olive oil
- 1 ½ teaspoons kosher salt
- 1 teaspoon garlic powder
- ½ teaspoon dried thyme leaves
- ½ teaspoon freshly ground black pepper

Directions:
1. Preheat the toaster oven to 350°F. Spray a 12 x 12-inch baking pan with nonstick cooking spray.
2. Drizzle the chicken cavity with about half of the lemon juice. Place half of the juiced lemon into the chicken cavity. Truss the chicken using kitchen twine.
3. Rub the chicken evenly with the olive oil.
4. Stir the salt, garlic powder, lemon zest, thyme, and pepper in a small bowl. Using your fingertips, rub the seasonings evenly over the chicken. Place the chicken, breast side up, in the prepared pan. Drizzle with the remaining lemon juice.
5. Roast, uncovered, for 1 ¼ hours to 1 ½ hours, or until a meat thermometer registers 165°F. Let stand for 10 minutes before carving.

Chicken Hand Pies

Servings: 8
Cooking Time: 10 Minutes
Ingredients:
- ¾ cup chicken broth
- ¾ cup frozen mixed peas and carrots
- 1 cup cooked chicken, chopped
- 1 tablespoon cornstarch
- 1 tablespoon milk
- salt and pepper
- 1 8-count can organic flaky biscuits
- oil for misting or cooking spray

Directions:
1. In a medium saucepan, bring chicken broth to a boil. Stir in the frozen peas and carrots and air-fry for 5 minutes over medium heat. Stir in chicken.
2. Mix the cornstarch into the milk until it dissolves. Stir it into the simmering chicken broth mixture and cook just until thickened.
3. Remove from heat, add salt and pepper to taste, and let cool slightly.
4. Lay biscuits out on wax paper. Peel each biscuit apart in the middle to make 2 rounds so you have 16 rounds total. Using your hands or a rolling pin, flatten each biscuit round slightly to make it larger and thinner.
5. Divide chicken filling among 8 of the biscuit rounds. Place remaining biscuit rounds on top and press edges all around. Use the tines of a fork to crimp biscuit edges and make sure they are sealed well.
6. Spray both sides lightly with oil or cooking spray.
7. Cook in a single layer, 4 at a time, at 330°F for 10 minutes or until biscuit dough is cooked through and golden brown.

Pesto-crusted Chicken

Servings: 2
Cooking Time: 31 Minutes
Ingredients:
- Pesto:
- 1 cup fresh cilantro, parsley, and basil leaves
- 3 tablespoons nonfat plain yogurt
- ¼ cup pine nuts, walnut, or pecans
- 3 tablespoons grated Parmesan cheese
- 2 peeled garlic cloves
- 1 tablespoon lemon juice
- 3 tablespoons olive oil
- Salt and freshly ground black pepper to taste
- 2 skinless, boneless chicken breast halves

Directions:
1. Preheat the toaster oven to 450° F.
2. Blend the pesto ingredients in a blender or food processor until smooth. Set aside.
3. Place the chicken breast halves in an oiled or nonstick

8½ × 8½ × 2-inch square (cake) pan. With a butter knife or spatula, spread the mixture liberally on both sides of each chicken breast. Cover the dish with aluminum foil.
4. BAKE, covered, for 25 minutes, or until the chicken is tender. Remove from the oven and uncover.
5. BROIL for 6 minutes, or until the pesto coating is lightly browned.

Sesame Chicken Breasts

Servings: 2
Cooking Time: 20 Minutes
Ingredients:
- Mixture:
- 2 tablespoons sesame oil
- 2 teaspoons soy sauce
- 2 teaspoons balsamic vinegar
- 2 skinless, boneless chicken breast filets
- 3 tablespoons sesame seeds

Directions:
1. Combine the mixture ingredients in a small bowl and brush the filets liberally. Reserve the mixture. Place the filets on a broiling rack with a pan underneath.
2. BROIL 15 minutes, or until the meat is tender and the juices, when the meat is pierced, run clear. Remove from the oven and brush the filets with the remaining mixture. Place the sesame seeds on a plate and press the chicken breast halves into the seeds, coating well.
3. BROIL for 5 minutes, or until the sesame seeds are browned.

Italian Baked Chicken

Servings: 4
Cooking Time: 28 Minutes
Ingredients:
- 1 pound boneless, skinless chicken breasts
- ½ cup dry white wine
- 3 tablespoons olive oil
- 2 tablespoons white wine vinegar
- 2 tablespoons fresh lemon juice
- 2 teaspoons Italian seasoning
- 3 cloves garlic, minced
- ½ teaspoon kosher salt
- ¼ teaspoon freshly ground black pepper
- 4 slices salami, cut in half
- 3 tablespoons shredded Parmesan cheese

Directions:
1. If the chicken breasts are large and thick, slice each breast in half lengthwise. Place the chicken in a shallow baking dish.
2. Combine the white wine, olive oil, vinegar, lemon juice, Italian seasoning, garlic, salt, and pepper in a small bowl. Pour over the chicken breasts. Cover and refrigerate for 2 to 8 hours, turning the chicken occasionally to coat.

3. Preheat the toaster oven to 375 °F.

4. Drain the chicken, discarding the marinade, and place the chicken in an ungreased 12 x 12-inch baking pan. Bake, uncovered, for 20 to 25 minutes or until the chicken is done and a meat thermometer registers 165 °F. Place one slice salami (two pieces) on top of each piece of the chicken. Sprinkle the Parmesan evenly over the chicken breasts and broil for 2 to 3 minutes, or until the cheese is melted and starting to brown.

Chicken Breast With Chermoula Sauce

Servings: 4
Cooking Time: 15 Minutes
Ingredients:
• Chicken Ingredients
• 2 boneless skinless chicken breasts 1 tablespoon olive oil
• 1 teaspoon salt
• 1 teaspoon pepper
• Chermoula Ingredients
• 1 cup fresh cilantro
• 1 cup fresh parsley
• ¼ cup fresh mint
• ½ teaspoon red chili flakes
• ½ teaspoon cumin seeds
• ½ teaspoon coriander seeds
• 3 garlic cloves, peeled
• ½ cup extra virgin olive oil
• 1 lemon, zested and juiced
• ¾ teaspoons smoked paprika
• ¾ teaspoons salt

Directions:
1. Combine all the chermoula sauce ingredients in a blender or food processor. Pulse until smooth. Taste and add salt if needed. Place into a bowl and set aside.
2. Slice the chicken breast in half lengthwise and lightly pound with a meat tenderizer until both halves are about
3. ½-inch thick.
4. Preheat the toaster oven to 430°F.
5. Line the food tray with foil, then place the chicken breasts on the tray. Drizzle chicken with olive oil and season with salt and pepper.
6. Insert the food tray at top position in the preheated oven.
7. Select the Air Fry function, adjust time to 15 minutes, and press Start/Pause.
8. Remove when the chicken breast reaches an internal temperature of 160°F. Allow the chicken to rest for 5 minutes.
9. Brush the chermoula sauce over the chicken, or serve chicken with chermoula sauce on the side.

Tandoori Chicken Legs

Servings: 2
Cooking Time: 30 Minutes
Ingredients:
• 1 cup plain yogurt
• 2 cloves garlic, minced
• 1 tablespoon grated fresh ginger
• 2 teaspoons paprika
• 2 teaspoons ground coriander
• 1 teaspoon ground turmeric
• 1 teaspoon salt
• ¼ teaspoon ground cayenne pepper
• juice of 1 lime
• 2 bone-in, skin-on chicken legs
• fresh cilantro leaves

Directions:
1. Make the marinade by combining the yogurt, garlic, ginger, spices and lime juice. Make slashes into the chicken legs to help the marinade penetrate the meat. Pour the marinade over the chicken legs, cover and let the chicken marinate for at least an hour or overnight in the refrigerator.
2. Preheat the toaster oven oven to 380°F.
3. Transfer the chicken legs from the marinade to the air fryer oven, reserving any extra marinade. Air-fry for 15 minutes. Flip the chicken over and pour the remaining marinade over the top. Air-fry for another 15 minutes, watching to make sure it doesn't brown too much. If it does start to get too brown, you can loosely tent the chicken with aluminum foil, tucking the ends of the foil under the chicken to stop it from blowing around.
4. Serve over rice with some fresh cilantro on top.

Quick Chicken For Filling

Servings: 2
Cooking Time: 8 Minutes
Ingredients:
• 1 pound chicken tenders, skinless and boneless
• ½ teaspoon ground cumin
• ½ teaspoon garlic powder
• cooking spray
Directions:
1. Sprinkle raw chicken tenders with seasonings.
2. Spray air fryer oven lightly with cooking spray to prevent sticking.
3. Place chicken in air fryer oven in single layer.
4. Air-fry at 390°F for 4 minutes, turn chicken strips over, and air-fry for an additional 4 minutes.
5. Test for doneness. Thick tenders may require an additional minute or two.

Chicken Adobo

Servings: 6
Cooking Time: 12 Minutes
Ingredients:
- 6 boneless chicken thighs
- ¼ cup soy sauce or tamari
- ½ cup rice wine vinegar
- 4 cloves garlic, minced
- ⅛ teaspoon crushed red pepper flakes
- ½ teaspoon black pepper

Directions:
1. Place the chicken thighs into a resealable plastic bag with the soy sauce or tamari, the rice wine vinegar, the garlic, and the crushed red pepper flakes. Seal the bag and let the chicken marinate at least 1 hour in the refrigerator.
2. Preheat the toaster oven to 400°F.
3. Drain the chicken and pat dry with a paper towel. Season the chicken with black pepper and liberally spray with cooking spray.
4. Place the chicken in the air fryer oven and air-fry for 9 minutes, turn over at 9 minutes and check for an internal temperature of 165°F, and cook another 3 minutes.

Chicken Wellington

Servings: 4
Cooking Time: 30 Minutes
Ingredients:
- 2 small (5- to 6-ounce) boneless, skinless chicken breast halves
- Kosher salt and freshly ground black pepper
- 2 teaspoons Italian seasoning
- 2 tablespoons olive oil
- 3 tablespoons unsalted butter, softened
- 3 ounces cream cheese, softened (about ⅓ cup)
- ¾ cup shredded Monterey Jack cheese
- ¼ cup grated Parmesan cheese
- 1 cup frozen (loose-pack) chopped spinach, thawed and squeezed dry
- ¾ cup chopped canned artichoke hearts, drained
- ½ teaspoon garlic powder
- 1 sheet frozen puff pastry, about 9 inches square, thawed (½ of a 17.3-ounce package)
- 1 large egg, lightly beaten

Directions:
1. Preheat the toaster oven to 425° F. Line a 12 x 12-inch baking pan with parchment paper.
2. Cut the chicken breasts in half lengthwise. Season each piece with the salt, pepper, and Italian seasoning. Fold the thinner end under the larger piece to make the chicken breasts into a rounded shape. Secure with toothpicks.
3. Heat a large skillet over medium-high heat. Add the olive oil and heat. Add the chicken breasts and brown well, turning to brown evenly. Remove from the skillet and set aside to cool. Remove the toothpicks.
4. Stir the butter, cream cheese, Monterey Jack, and Parmesan in a large bowl. Stir in the spinach, artichoke hearts, and garlic powder. Season with salt and pepper.
5. Roll out the puff pastry sheet on a lightly floured board until it makes a 12-inch square. Cut into four equal pieces. Spread one-fourth of the spinach-artichoke mixture on the surface of each pastry square to within ½ inch of all four edges. Place the chicken in the center of each. Gently fold the puff pastry up over the chicken and pinch the edges to seal tightly.
6. Place each chicken bundle, seam side down, on the prepared pan. Brush the top of each bundle lightly with the beaten egg. Bake for 25 to 30 minutes, or until the pastry is golden brown and crisp and a meat thermometer inserted into the chicken reaches 165°F.

Chicken Potpie

Servings: 4
Cooking Time: 48 Minutes
Ingredients:
- Pie filling:
- 1 tablespoon unbleached flour
- ½ cup evaporated skim milk
- 4 skinless, boneless chicken thighs, cut into 1-inch cubes
- 1 cup potatoes, peeled and cut into ½-inch pieces
- ½ cup frozen green peas
- ½ cup thinly sliced carrot
- 2 tablespoons chopped onion
- ½ cup chopped celery
- 1 teaspoon garlic powder
- Salt and freshly ground black pepper to taste
- 8 sheets phyllo pastry, thawed Olive oil

Directions:
1. Preheat the toaster oven to 400° F.
2. Whisk the flour into the milk until smooth in a 1-quart 8½ × 8½ × 4-inch ovenproof baking dish. Add the remaining filling ingredients and mix well. Adjust the seasonings to taste. Cover the dish with aluminum foil.
3. BAKE for 40 minutes, or until the carrot, potatoes, and celery are tender. Remove from the oven and uncover.
4. Place one sheet of phyllo pastry on top of the baked pie-filling mixture, bending the edges to fit the shape of the baking dish. Brush the sheet with olive oil. Add another sheet on top of it and brush with oil. Continue adding the remaining sheets, brushing each one, until the crust is completed. Brush the top with oil.
5. BAKE for 6 minutes, or until the phyllo pastry is browned.

Chicken Fajitas

Servings: 4
Cooking Time: 15 Minutes
Ingredients:
- FOR THE FAJITAS
- ½ teaspoon ground cumin
- ½ teaspoon garlic powder
- ¼ teaspoon smoked paprika
- ¼ teaspoon onion powder
- ¼ teaspoon chili powder
- 1 pound boneless, skinless chicken breast, cut into ¼-inch strips
- 1 red bell pepper, cut into thin slices
- 1 green bell pepper, cut into thin slices
- 1 small red onion, cut into thin slices
- 2 tablespoons olive oil
- 8 (6-inch) tortillas
- OPTIONAL TOPPINGS
- Salsa
- Sour cream
- Pickled jalapeños
- Shredded lettuce

Directions:
1. Preheat the toaster oven to 375°F on AIR FRY for 5 minutes.
2. Place the air-fryer basket in the baking tray.
3. In a large bowl, stir the cumin, garlic powder, paprika, onion powder, and chili powder until well mixed. Add the chicken, bell peppers, onion, and oil, and toss to coat evenly.
4. Spread the chicken and veggies on the baking sheet.
5. In position 2, air fry for 15 minutes, tossing them halfway through, until cooked and the vegetables are lightly browned.
6. Serve tucked into the tortillas with your favorite toppings.

Crispy Chicken Tenders

Servings: 4
Cooking Time: 22 Minutes
Ingredients:
- 1 pound boneless, skinless chicken breasts
- ½ cup all-purpose flour
- ½ teaspoon kosher salt
- ¼ teaspoon freshly ground black ground pepper
- 1 large egg, beaten
- 3 tablespoons whole milk
- 1 cup cornflake crumbs
- ½ cup grated Parmesan cheese
- Nonstick cooking spray

Directions:
1. Preheat the toaster oven to 375°F. Line a 12 x 12-inch baking pan with nonstick aluminum foil. (Or if lining the pan with regular foil, spray it with nonstick cooking spray.)
2. Cover the chicken with plastic wrap. Pound the chicken with the flat side of a meat pounder until it is even and about ½ inch thick. Cut the chicken into strips about 1 by 3 inches.
3. Combine the flour, salt, and pepper in a small shallow dish. Place the egg and milk in another small shallow dish and use a fork to combine. Place the cornflake crumbs and Parmesan in a third small shallow dish and combine.
4. Dredge each chicken piece in the flour, then dip in the egg mixture, and then coat with the cornflake crumb mixture. Place the chicken strips in a single layer in the prepared baking pan. Spray the chicken strips generously with nonstick cooking spray.
5. Bake for 10 minutes. Turn the chicken and spray with nonstick cooking spray. Bake for an additional 10 to 12 minutes, or until crisp and a meat thermometer registers 165 °F.

Golden Seasoned Chicken Wings

Servings: 2
Cooking Time: 40 Minutes
Ingredients:
- Oil spray (hand-pumped)
- ¾ cup all-purpose flour
- 1 teaspoon garlic powder
- 1 teaspoon smoked paprika
- ½ teaspoon sea salt
- ¼ teaspoon freshly ground black pepper
- ¼ teaspoon onion powder
- 2 pounds chicken wing drumettes and flats

Directions:
1. Preheat the toaster oven to 400°F on AIR FRY for 5 minutes.
2. Place the air-fryer basket in the baking tray and spray it generously with the oil.
3. In a medium bowl, stir the flour, garlic powder, paprika, sea salt, pepper, and onion powder until well mixed.
4. Add half the chicken wings to the bowl and toss to coat with the flour.
5. Arrange the wings in the basket and spray both sides lightly with the oil.
6. In position 2, air fry for 20 minutes, turning halfway through, until golden brown and crispy.
7. Repeat with the remaining wings, covering the cooked wings loosely with foil to keep them warm. Serve.

Chicken Parmesan

Servings: 4
Cooking Time: 11 Minutes

Ingredients:

- 4 chicken tenders
- Italian seasoning
- salt
- ¼ cup cornstarch
- ½ cup Italian salad dressing
- ¼ cup panko breadcrumbs
- ¼ cup grated Parmesan cheese, plus more for serving
- oil for misting or cooking spray
- 8 ounces spaghetti, cooked
- 1 24-ounce jar marinara sauce

Directions:

1. Pound chicken tenders with meat mallet or rolling pin until about ¼-inch thick.
2. Sprinkle both sides with Italian seasoning and salt to taste.
3. Place cornstarch and salad dressing in 2 separate shallow dishes.
4. In a third shallow dish, mix together the panko crumbs and Parmesan cheese.
5. Dip flattened chicken in cornstarch, then salad dressing. Dip in the panko mixture, pressing into the chicken so the coating sticks well.
6. Spray both sides with oil or cooking spray. Place in air fryer oven in single layer.
7. Air-fry at 390°F for 5 minutes. Spray with oil again, turning chicken to coat both sides. See tip about turning.
8. Air-fry for an additional 6 minutes or until chicken juices run clear and outside is browned.
9. While chicken is cooking, heat marinara sauce and stir into cooked spaghetti.
10. To serve, divide spaghetti with sauce among 4 dinner plates, and top each with a fried chicken tender. Pass additional Parmesan at the table for those who want extra cheese.

Thai Chicken Drumsticks

Servings: 4
Cooking Time: 20 Minutes

Ingredients:

- 2 tablespoons soy sauce
- ¼ cup rice wine vinegar
- 2 tablespoons chili garlic sauce
- 2 tablespoons sesame oil
- 1 teaspoon minced fresh ginger
- 2 teaspoons sugar
- ½ teaspoon ground coriander
- juice of 1 lime
- 8 chicken drumsticks (about 2½ pounds)
- ¼ cup chopped peanuts
- chopped fresh cilantro
- lime wedges

Directions:

1. Combine the soy sauce, rice wine vinegar, chili sauce, sesame oil, ginger, sugar, coriander and lime juice in a large bowl and mix together. Add the chicken drumsticks and marinate for 30 minutes.
2. Preheat the toaster oven to 370°F.
3. Place the chicken in the air fryer oven. It's ok if the ends of the drumsticks overlap a little. Spoon half of the marinade over the chicken, and reserve the other half.
4. Air-fry for 10 minutes. Turn the chicken over and pour the rest of the marinade over the chicken. Air-fry for an additional 10 minutes.
5. Transfer the chicken to a plate to rest and cool to an edible temperature. Pour the marinade from the bottom of the air fryer oven into a small saucepan and bring it to a simmer over medium-high heat. Simmer the liquid for 2 minutes so that it thickens enough to coat the back of a spoon.
6. Transfer the chicken to a serving platter, pour the sauce over the chicken and sprinkle the chopped peanuts on top. Garnish with chopped cilantro and lime wedges.

Hot Thighs

Servings: 4
Cooking Time: 40 Minutes

Ingredients:

- 6 skinless, boneless chicken thighs
- ¼ cup fresh lemon juice
- Seasonings:
- 1 teaspoon garlic powder
- ¼ teaspoon cayenne
- ½ teaspoon chili powder
- 1 teaspoon onion powder
- Salt and freshly ground black pepper to taste

Directions:

1. Preheat the toaster oven to 450° F.
2. Brush the chicken thighs liberally with the lemon juice. Set aside.
3. Combine the seasonings in a small bowl and transfer to a paper or plastic bag. Add the thighs and shake well to coat. Remove from the bag and place in an oiled or nonstick 8½ × 8½ × 2-inch square (cake) pan. Cover the pan with aluminum foil.
4. BAKE, covered, for 20 minutes. Turn the pieces with tongs and bake again for another 20 minutes, or until the meat is tender and lightly browned.

Chicken Souvlaki Gyros

Servings: 4
Cooking Time: 18 Minutes
Ingredients:
- ¼ cup extra-virgin olive oil
- 1 clove garlic, crushed
- 1 tablespoon Italian seasoning
- ½ teaspoon paprika
- ½ lemon, sliced
- ¼ teaspoon salt
- 1 pound boneless, skinless chicken breasts
- 4 whole-grain pita breads
- 1 cup shredded lettuce
- ½ cup chopped tomatoes
- ¼ cup chopped red onion
- ¼ cup cucumber yogurt sauce

Directions:
1. In a large resealable plastic bag, combine the olive oil, garlic, Italian seasoning, paprika, lemon, and salt. Add the chicken to the bag and secure shut. Vigorously shake until all the ingredients are combined. Set in the fridge for 2 hours to marinate.
2. When ready to cook, preheat the toaster oven to 360°F.
3. Liberally spray the air fryer oven with olive oil mist. Remove the chicken from the bag and discard the leftover marinade. Place the chicken into the air fryer oven, allowing enough room between the chicken breasts to flip.
4. Air-fry for 10 minutes, flip, and cook another 8 minutes.
5. Remove the chicken from the air fryer oven when it has cooked (or the internal temperature of the chicken reaches 165°F). Let rest 5 minutes. Then thinly slice the chicken into strips.
6. Assemble the gyros by placing the pita bread on a flat surface and topping with chicken, lettuce, tomatoes, onion, and a drizzle of yogurt sauce.
7. Serve warm.

Chicken Cutlets With Broccoli Rabe And Roasted Peppers

Servings: 2
Cooking Time: 10 Minutes
Ingredients:
- ½ bunch broccoli rabe
- olive oil, in a spray bottle
- salt and freshly ground black pepper
- ⅔ cup roasted red pepper strips
- 2 (4-ounce) boneless, skinless chicken breasts
- 2 tablespoons all-purpose flour
- 1 egg, beaten
- ⅓ cup seasoned breadcrumbs
- 2 slices aged provolone cheese

Directions:
1. Bring a medium saucepot of salted water to a boil on the stovetop. Blanch the broccoli rabe for 3 minutes in the boiling water and then drain. When it has cooled a little, squeeze out as much water as possible, drizzle a little olive oil on top, season with salt and black pepper and set aside. Dry the roasted red peppers with a clean kitchen towel and set them aside as well.
2. Place each chicken breast between 2 pieces of plastic wrap. Use a meat pounder to flatten the chicken breasts to about ½-inch thick. Season the chicken on both sides with salt and pepper.
3. Preheat the toaster oven to 400°F.
4. Set up a dredging station with three shallow dishes. Place the flour in one dish, the egg in a second dish and the breadcrumbs in a third dish. Coat the chicken on all sides with the flour. Shake off any excess flour and dip the chicken into the egg. Let the excess egg drip off and coat both sides of the chicken in the breadcrumbs. Spray the chicken with olive oil on both sides and transfer to the air fryer oven.
5. Air-fry the chicken at 400°F for 5 minutes. Turn the chicken over and air-fry for another minute. Then, top the chicken breast with the broccoli rabe and roasted peppers. Place a slice of the provolone cheese on top and secure it with a toothpick or two.
6. Air-fry at 360° for 3 to 4 minutes to melt the cheese and warm everything together.

Italian Roasted Chicken Thighs

Servings: 6
Cooking Time: 14 Minutes
Ingredients:
- 6 boneless chicken thighs
- ½ teaspoon dried oregano
- ½ teaspoon garlic powder
- ½ teaspoon sea salt
- ½ teaspoon black pepper
- ¼ teaspoon crushed red pepper flakes

Directions:
1. Pat the chicken thighs with paper towel.
2. In a small bowl, mix the oregano, garlic powder, salt, pepper, and crushed red pepper flakes. Rub the spice mixture onto the chicken thighs.
3. Preheat the toaster oven to 400°F.
4. Place the chicken thighs in the air fryer oven and spray with cooking spray. Air-fry for 10 minutes, turn over, and cook another 4 minutes. When cooking completes, the internal temperature should read 165°F.

Gluten-free Nutty Chicken Fingers

Servings: 4

Cooking Time: 10 Minutes

Ingredients:
- ½ cup gluten-free flour
- ½ teaspoon garlic powder
- ¼ teaspoon onion powder
- ¼ teaspoon black pepper
- ¼ teaspoon salt
- 1 cup walnuts, pulsed into coarse flour
- ½ cup gluten-free breadcrumbs
- 2 large eggs
- 1 pound boneless, skinless chicken tenders

Directions:
1. Preheat the toaster oven to 400°F.
2. In a medium bowl, mix the flour, garlic, onion, pepper, and salt. Set aside.
3. In a separate bowl, mix the walnut flour and breadcrumbs.
4. In a third bowl, whisk the eggs.
5. Liberally spray the air fryer oven with olive oil spray.
6. Pat the chicken tenders dry with a paper towel. Dredge the tenders one at a time in the flour, then dip them in the egg, and toss them in the breadcrumb coating. Repeat until all tenders are coated.
7. Set each tender in the air fryer oven, leaving room on each side of the tender to allow for flipping.
8. When the air fryer oven is full, cook 5 minutes, flip, and cook another 5 minutes. Check the internal temperature after cooking completes; it should read 165°F. If it does not, cook another 2 to 4 minutes.
9. Remove the tenders and let cool 5 minutes before serving. Repeat until all the tenders are cooked.

Poblano Bake

Servings: 4

Cooking Time: 11 Minutes

Ingredients:
- 2 large poblano peppers (approx. 5½ inches long excluding stem)
- ¾ pound ground turkey, raw
- ¾ cup cooked brown rice
- 1 teaspoon chile powder
- ½ teaspoon ground cumin
- ½ teaspoon garlic powder
- 4 ounces sharp Cheddar cheese, grated
- 1 8-ounce jar salsa, warmed

Directions:
1. Slice each pepper in half lengthwise so that you have four wide, flat pepper halves.
2. Remove seeds and membrane and discard. Rinse inside and out.
3. In a large bowl, combine turkey, rice, chile powder, cumin, and garlic powder. Mix well.
4. Divide turkey filling into 4 portions and stuff one into each of the 4 pepper halves. Press lightly to pack down.
5. Place 2 pepper halves in air fryer oven and air-fry at 390°F for 10 minutes or until turkey is well done.
6. Top each pepper half with ¼ of the grated cheese. Cook 1 more minute or just until cheese melts.
7. Repeat steps 5 and 6 to cook remaining pepper halves.
8. To serve, place each pepper half on a plate and top with ¼ cup warm salsa.

Chicken Nuggets

Servings: 20

Cooking Time: 14 Minutes

Ingredients:
- 1 pound boneless, skinless chicken thighs, cut into 1-inch chunks
- ¾ teaspoon salt
- ½ teaspoon black pepper
- ½ teaspoon garlic powder
- ½ teaspoon onion powder
- ½ cup flour
- 2 eggs, beaten
- ½ cup panko breadcrumbs
- 3 tablespoons plain breadcrumbs
- oil for misting or cooking spray

Directions:
1. In the bowl of a food processor, combine chicken, ½ teaspoon salt, pepper, garlic powder, and onion powder. Process in short pulses until chicken is very finely chopped and well blended.
2. Place flour in one shallow dish and beaten eggs in another. In a third dish or plastic bag, mix together the panko crumbs, plain breadcrumbs, and ¼ teaspoon salt.
3. Shape chicken mixture into small nuggets. Dip nuggets in flour, then eggs, then panko crumb mixture.
4. Spray nuggets on both sides with oil or cooking spray and place in air fryer oven in a single layer, close but not overlapping.
5. Air-fry at 360°F for 10 minutes. Spray with oil and cook 4 minutes, until chicken is done and coating is golden brown.
6. Repeat step 5 to cook remaining nuggets.

Marinated Green Pepper And Pineapple Chicken

Servings: 4
Cooking Time: 20 Minutes
Ingredients:
- Marinade:
- 1 teaspoon finely chopped fresh ginger
- 2 garlic cloves, finely chopped
- 1 teaspoon toasted sesame oil
- 1 tablespoon brown sugar
- 2 tablespoons soy sauce
- ¾ cup dry white wine
- 2 skinless, boneless chicken breasts, cut into 1 × 3-inch strips
- 2 tablespoons chopped onion
- 1 bell pepper, chopped
- 1 5-ounce can pineapple chunks, drained
- 2 tablespoons grated unsweetened coconut

Directions:
1. Combine the marinade ingredients in a medium bowl and blend well. Add the chicken strips and spoon the mixture over them. Marinate in the refrigerator for at least 1 hour. Remove the strips from the marinade and place in an oiled or nonstick 8½ × 8½ × 2-inch square (cake) pan. Add the onion and pepper and mix well.
2. BROIL for 8 minutes. Then remove from the oven and, using tongs, turn the chicken, pepper, and onion pieces. (Spoon the reserved marinade over the pieces, if desired.)
3. BROIL again for 8 minutes, or until the chicken, pepper, and onion are cooked through and tender. Add the pineapple chunks and coconut and toss to mix well.
4. BROIL for another 4 minutes, or until the coconut is lightly browned.

Crispy Chicken Parmesan

Servings: 4
Cooking Time: 12 Minutes
Ingredients:
- 4 skinless, boneless chicken breasts, pounded thin to ¼-inch thickness
- 1 teaspoon salt, divided
- ½ teaspoon black pepper, divided
- 1 cup flour
- 2 eggs
- 1 cup panko breadcrumbs
- ½ teaspoon dried oregano
- ½ cup grated Parmesan cheese

Directions:
1. Pat the chicken breasts with a paper towel. Season the chicken with ½ teaspoon of the salt and ¼ teaspoon of the pepper.
2. In a medium bowl, place the flour.
3. In a second bowl, whisk the eggs.
4. In a third bowl, place the breadcrumbs, oregano, cheese, and the remaining ½ teaspoon of salt and ¼ teaspoon of pepper.
5. Dredge the chicken in the flour and shake off the excess. Dip the chicken into the eggs and then into the breadcrumbs. Set the chicken on a plate and repeat with the remaining chicken pieces.
6. Preheat the toaster oven to 360°F.
7. Place the chicken in the air fryer oven and spray liberally with cooking spray. Air-fry for 8 minutes, turn the chicken breasts over, and cook another 4 minutes. When golden brown, check for an internal temperature of 165°F.

Teriyaki Chicken Drumsticks

Servings: 2
Cooking Time: 17 Minutes
Ingredients:
- 2 tablespoons soy sauce
- ¼ cup dry sherry
- 1 tablespoon brown sugar
- 2 tablespoons water
- 1 tablespoon rice wine vinegar
- 1 clove garlic, crushed
- 1-inch fresh ginger, peeled and sliced
- pinch crushed red pepper flakes
- 4 to 6 bone-in, skin-on chicken drumsticks
- 1 tablespoon cornstarch
- fresh cilantro leaves

Directions:
1. Make the marinade by combining the soy sauce, dry sherry, brown sugar, water, rice vinegar, garlic, ginger and crushed red pepper flakes. Pour the marinade over the chicken legs, cover and let the chicken marinate for 1 to 4 hours in the refrigerator.
2. Preheat the toaster oven to 380°F.
3. Transfer the chicken from the marinade to the air fryer oven, transferring any extra marinade to a small saucepan. Air-fry at 380°F for 8 minutes. Flip the chicken over and continue to air-fry for another 6 minutes, watching to make sure it doesn't brown too much.
4. While the chicken is cooking, bring the reserved marinade to a simmer on the stovetop. Dissolve the cornstarch in 2 tablespoons of water and stir this into the saucepan. Bring to a boil to thicken the sauce. Remove the garlic clove and slices of ginger from the sauce and set aside.
5. When the time is up on the air fryer oven, brush the thickened sauce on the chicken and air-fry for 3 more minutes. Remove the chicken from the air fryer oven and brush with the remaining sauce.
6. Serve over rice and sprinkle the cilantro leaves on top.

Guiltless Bacon

Servings: 4
Cooking Time: 10 Minutes
Ingredients:
• 6 slices lean turkey bacon, placed on a broiling pan
Directions:
1. BROIL 5 minutes, turn the pieces, and broil again for 5 more minutes, or until done to your preference. Press the slices between paper towels and serve immediately.

Tandoori Chicken

Servings: 4
Cooking Time: 30 Minutes
Ingredients:
• 1 cup plain Greek yogurt
• ¼ sweet onion, finely chopped
• 2 teaspoons garam masala
• 1 teaspoon minced garlic
• 1 teaspoon fresh ginger, peeled and grated
• ½ teaspoon ground cumin
• ½ teaspoon ground coriander
• ¼ teaspoon sea salt
• ⅛ teaspoon cayenne powder
• 4 (4-ounce) skinless, boneless chicken breasts
• Oil spray (hand-pumped)
Directions:
1. Preheat the toaster oven to 375°F on AIR FRY for 5 minutes.
2. In a medium bowl, whisk the yogurt, onion, garam masala, garlic, ginger, cumin, coriander, salt, and cayenne until well blended. Add the chicken breast, turning to coat.
3. Cover the bowl and refrigerate for at least 3 hours to overnight.
4. Place the air-fryer basket in the baking tray and spray it generously with the oil.
5. Place the chicken breasts in the basket after shaking off the excess marinade. Discard the remaining marinade.
6. In position 2, air fry for 25 to 30 minutes, turning halfway through, until browned with an internal temperature of 165°F. Serve.

I Forgot To Thaw—garlic Capered Chicken Thighs

Servings: 4
Cooking Time: 50 Minutes
Ingredients:
• 6 frozen skinless, boneless chicken thighs
• Garlic mixture:
• 3 garlic cloves, minced
• ¾ cup dry white wine
• 2 tablespoons capers
• ½ teaspoon paprika
• ¼ teaspoon ground cumin
• Salt and freshly ground black pepper to taste
Directions:
1. Preheat the toaster oven to 400° F.
2. Thaw the chicken as directed. Separate the pieces and add the garlic mixture, which has been combined in a small bowl, stirring well to coat. Cover the dish with aluminum foil.
3. BAKE for 30 minutes, or until the chicken is tender. Remove the cover and turn the chicken pieces, spooning the sauce over them.
4. BROIL for 8 minutes, or until the chicken is lightly browned.

Beef Pork And Lamb

Beef Pork And Lamb

Glazed Meatloaf

Servings: 4
Cooking Time: 60 Minutes
Ingredients:
- 2 pounds extra-lean ground beef
- ½ cup fine bread crumbs
- 1 large egg
- 1 medium carrot, shredded
- 2 teaspoons minced garlic
- ¼ cup milk
- 1 tablespoon Italian seasoning
- ½ teaspoon sea salt
- ⅛ teaspoon freshly ground black pepper
- ½ cup ketchup
- 1 tablespoon dark brown sugar
- 1 teaspoon apple cider vinegar

Directions:
1. Place the rack in position 1 and preheat the toaster oven to 375°F on BAKE for 5 minutes.
2. In a large bowl, mix the ground beef, bread crumbs, egg, carrot, garlic, milk, Italian seasoning, salt, and pepper until well combined.
3. Press the mixture into a 9-by-5-inch loaf pan.
4. In a small bowl, stir the ketchup, brown sugar, and vinegar. Set aside.
5. Bake for 40 minutes.
6. Take the meatloaf out and spread the glaze over the top. Bake an additional 20 minutes until cooked through, with an internal temperature of 165°F. Serve.

Albóndigas

Servings: 4
Cooking Time: 15 Minutes
Ingredients:
- 1 pound Lean ground pork
- 3 tablespoons Very finely chopped trimmed scallions
- 3 tablespoons Finely chopped fresh cilantro leaves
- 3 tablespoons Plain panko bread crumbs (gluten-free, if a concern)
- 3 tablespoons Dry white wine, dry sherry, or unsweetened apple juice
- 1½ teaspoons Minced garlic
- 1¼ teaspoons Mild smoked paprika
- ¾ teaspoon Dried oregano
- ¾ teaspoon Table salt
- ¼ teaspoon Ground black pepper
- Olive oil spray

Directions:

1. Preheat the toaster oven to 400°F.
2. Mix the ground pork, scallions, cilantro, bread crumbs, wine or its substitute, garlic, smoked paprika, oregano, salt, and pepper in a bowl until the herbs and spices are evenly distributed in the mixture.
3. Lightly coat your clean hands with olive oil spray, then form the ground pork mixture into balls, using 2 tablespoons for each one. Spray your hands frequently so that the meat mixture doesn't stick.
4. Set the balls in the air fryer oven so that they're not touching, even if they're close together. Air-fry undisturbed for 15 minutes, or until well browned and an instant-read meat thermometer inserted into one or two balls registers 165°F.
5. Use a nonstick-safe spatula and kitchen tongs for balance to gently transfer the fragile balls to a wire rack to cool for 5 minutes before serving.

Beer-baked Pork Tenderloin

Servings: 4
Cooking Time: 40 Minutes
Ingredients:
- 1 pound lean pork tenderloin, fat trimmed off
- 3 garlic cloves, minced
- 1 cup good-quality dark ale or beer
- 2 bay leaves
- Salt and freshly cracked black pepper
- Spiced apple slices

Directions:
1. Preheat the toaster oven to 400° F.
2. Place the tenderloin in an 8½ × 8½ × 4-inch ovenproof baking dish. Sprinkle the minced garlic over the pork, pour over the beer, add the bay leaves, and season to taste with the salt and pepper. Cover with aluminum foil.
3. BAKE, covered, for 40 minutes, or until the meat is tender. Discard the bay leaves and serve sliced with the liquid. Garnish with the spiced apple slices.

Pretzel-coated Pork Tenderloin

Servings: 4
Cooking Time: 10 Minutes
Ingredients:
- 1 Large egg white(s)
- 2 teaspoons Dijon mustard (gluten-free, if a concern)
- 1½ cups (about 6 ounces) Crushed pretzel crumbs
- 1 pound (4 sections) Pork tenderloin, cut into ¼-pound (4-ounce) sections
- Vegetable oil spray

Directions:

1. Preheat the toaster oven to 350°F .

2. Set up and fill two shallow soup plates or small pie plates on your counter: one for the egg white(s), whisked with the mustard until foamy; and one for the pretzel crumbs.

3. Dip a section of pork tenderloin in the egg white mixture and turn it to coat well, even on the ends. Let any excess egg white mixture slip back into the rest, then set the pork in the pretzel crumbs. Roll it several times, pressing gently, until the pork is evenly coated, even on the ends. Generously coat the pork section with vegetable oil spray, set it aside, and continue coating and spraying the remaining sections.

4. Set the pork sections in the air fryer oven with at least ¼ inch between them. Air-fry undisturbed for 10 minutes, or until an instant-read meat thermometer inserted into the center of one section registers 145°F.

5. Use kitchen tongs to transfer the pieces to a wire rack. Cool for 3 to 5 minutes before serving.

Chicken Fried Steak

Servings: 4

Cooking Time: 15 Minutes

Ingredients:
- 2 eggs
- ½ cup buttermilk
- 1½ cups flour
- ¾ teaspoon salt
- ½ teaspoon pepper
- 1 pound beef cube steaks
- salt and pepper
- oil for misting or cooking spray

Directions:

1. Beat together eggs and buttermilk in a shallow dish.

2. In another shallow dish, stir together the flour, ½ teaspoon salt, and ¼ teaspoon pepper.

3. Season cube steaks with remaining salt and pepper to taste. Dip in flour, buttermilk egg wash, and then flour again.

4. Spray both sides of steaks with oil or cooking spray.

5. Cooking in 2 batches, place steaks in air fryer oven in single layer. Air-fry at 360°F for 10 minutes. Spray tops of steaks with oil and cook 5 minutes or until meat is well done.

6. Repeat to cook remaining steaks.

Beef Bourguignon

Servings: 6

Cooking Time: 240 Minutes

Ingredients:
- 4 slices bacon, chopped into ½-inch pieces
- 3 pounds chuck roast, cut into 2-inch chunks
- 1 tablespoon kosher salt, plus more to taste
- 1½ tablespoons black pepper, plus more to taste
- 4 tablespoons all purpose flour, divided
- 2 tablespoons olive oil
- 2 large carrots, cut into ½-inch thick slices
- ½ large white onion, diced
- 4 cloves garlic, minced
- 2 tablespoons tomato paste
- 3 cups red wine (Merlot, Pinot Noir, or Chianti)
- 2 cups beef stock
- 1 beef bouillon cube, crushed
- ½ teaspoon dried thyme
- ¼ teaspoon dried parsley
- 2 bay leaves
- 10 ounces fresh small white or brown mushrooms, quartered
- 2 tablespoons cornstarch (optional)
- 2 tablespoons water (optional)

Directions:

1. Render the bacon in a large pot over medium heat for 5 minutes or until crispy.

2. Drain the bacon and set aside, leaving the bacon fat in the pot.

3. Mix together chuck roast chunks, kosher salt, black pepper, and 2 tablespoons of all purpose flour until well combined.

4. Dredge the beef of any extra flour and sear in the bacon grease for about 4 minutes on each side. It is important not to overcrowd the pot, so you may need to work in batches.

5. Remove the beef when done and set aside with the bacon.

6. Add the olive oil, sliced carrots, and diced onion to the pot. Cook for 5 minutes, then add the garlic and cook for another minute.

7. Add the tomato paste and cook for 1 minute, then mix in the remaining 2 tablespoons of flour and cook on medium low for 4 minutes.

8. Pour in the wine and beef stock, scraping the bottom of the pot to make sure there aren't any bits stuck to the bottom.

9. Add the bacon and seared meat back into the pot, along with the bouillon cube, dried thyme, dried parsley, bay leaves, and mushrooms. Mix well and bring to a light boil.

10. Insert the wire rack at low position in the Air Fryer Toaster Oven.

11. Cover the pot with foil and place on the rack in the oven. Make sure the foil is secure so it doesn't lift and contact the heating elements.

12. Select the Slow Cook function, adjust time to 4 hours, and press Start/Pause.

13. Remove the pot carefully from the oven when done and place back on the stove.

14. Discard the foil, mix the stew, and season to taste with salt and pepper.

15. Thicken the stew if desired by using a cornstarch slurry

of 2 tablespoons cornstarch and 2 tablespoons water. Add half, mix, and bring to a boil, stirring occasionally. If the sauce is still too thin, add the other half of the slurry.

Barbecued Broiled Pork Chops

Servings: 2
Cooking Time: 16 Minutes
Ingredients:
- Barbecue sauce mixture:
- 1 tablespoon ketchup
- ¼ cup dry red wine
- 1 tablespoon vegetable oil
- ⅛ teaspoon smoked flavoring (liquid smoke)
- 1 teaspoon chili powder
- 1 teaspoon ground cumin
- 1 teaspoon brown sugar
- ¼ teaspoon butcher's pepper
- 2 large (6- to 8-ounce) lean pork chops, approximately ¾ to 1 inch thick

Directions:
1. Combine the barbecue sauce mixture ingredients in a small bowl. Brush the chops with the sauce and place on a broiling rack with a pan underneath.
2. BROIL 8 minutes, turn with tongs, and broil for another 8 minutes, or until the meat is cooked to your preference.

Crispy Smoked Pork Chops

Servings: 3
Cooking Time: 8 Minutes
Ingredients:
- ⅔ cup All-purpose flour or tapioca flour
- 1 Large egg white(s)
- 2 tablespoons Water
- 1½ cups Corn flake crumbs (gluten-free, if a concern)
- 3 ½-pound, ½-inch-thick bone-in smoked pork chops

Directions:
1. Preheat the toaster oven to 375°F.
2. Set up and fill three shallow soup plates or small pie plates on your counter: one for the flour; one for the egg white(s), whisked with the water until foamy; and one for the corn flake crumbs.
3. Set a chop in the flour and turn it several times, coating both sides and the edges. Gently shake off any excess flour, then set it in the beaten egg white mixture. Turn to coat both sides as well as the edges. Let any excess egg white slip back into the rest, then set the chop in the corn flake crumbs. Turn it several times, pressing gently to coat the chop evenly on both sides and around the edge. Set the chop aside and continue coating the remaining chop(s) in the same way.
4. Set the chops in the air fryer oven with as much air space between them as possible. Air-fry undisturbed for 8 minutes, or until the coating is crunchy and the chops are

heated through.
5. Use kitchen tongs to transfer the chops to a wire rack and cool for a couple of minutes before serving.

Italian Meatballs

Servings: 4
Cooking Time: 12 Minutes
Ingredients:
- 12 ounces lean ground beef
- 4 ounces Italian sausage, casing removed
- ½ cup breadcrumbs
- 1 cup grated Parmesan cheese
- 1 egg
- 2 tablespoons milk
- 2 teaspoons Italian seasoning
- ½ teaspoon onion powder
- ½ teaspoon garlic powder
- Pinch of red pepper flakes

Directions:
1. In a large bowl, place all the ingredients and mix well. Roll out 24 meatballs.
2. Preheat the toaster oven to 360°F.
3. Place the meatballs in the air fryer oven and air-fry for 12 minutes, tossing every 4 minutes. Using a food thermometer, check to ensure the internal temperature of the meatballs is 165°F.

Lamb Burger With Feta And Olives

Servings: 3
Cooking Time: 16 Minutes
Ingredients:
- 2 teaspoons olive oil
- ⅓ onion, finely chopped
- 1 clove garlic, minced
- 1 pound ground lamb
- 2 tablespoons fresh parsley, finely chopped
- 1½ teaspoons fresh oregano, finely chopped
- ½ cup black olives, finely chopped
- ⅓ cup crumbled feta cheese
- ½ teaspoon salt
- freshly ground black pepper
- 4 thick pita breads
- toppings and condiments

Directions:
1. Preheat a medium skillet over medium-high heat on the stovetop. Add the olive oil and cook the onion until tender, but not browned – about 4 to 5 minutes. Add the garlic and air-fry for another minute. Transfer the onion and garlic to a mixing bowl and add the ground lamb, parsley, oregano, olives, feta cheese, salt and pepper. Gently mix the ingredients together.
2. Divide the mixture into 3 or 4 equal portions and then form the hamburgers, being careful not to over-handle the

meat. One good way to do this is to throw the meat back and forth between your hands like a baseball, packing the meat each time you catch it. Flatten the balls into patties, making an indentation in the center of each patty. Flatten the sides of the patties as well to make it easier to fit them into the air fryer oven.

3. Preheat the toaster oven to 370°F.

4. If you don't have room for all four burgers, air-fry two or three burgers at a time for 8 minutes at 370°F. Flip the burgers over and air-fry for another 8 minutes. If you cooked your burgers in batches, return the first batch of burgers to the air fryer oven for the last two minutes of cooking to reheat. This should give you a medium-well burger. If you'd prefer a medium-rare burger, shorten the cooking time to about 13 minutes. Remove the burgers to a resting plate and let the burgers rest for a few minutes before dressing and serving.

5. While the burgers are resting, toast the pita breads in the air fryer oven for 2 minutes. Tuck the burgers into the toasted pita breads, or wrap the pitas around the burgers and serve with a tzatziki sauce or some mayonnaise.

Herbed Lamb Burgers

Servings: 4
Cooking Time: 15 Minutes
Ingredients:
- 1 pound lean ground lamb
- 1 large egg
- 1 tablespoon fresh parsley, chopped
- 2 teaspoons fresh mint, chopped
- 1 teaspoon minced garlic
- ¼ teaspoon sea salt
- ⅛ teaspoon freshly ground black pepper
- Olive oil spray (hand-pumped)
- 4 whole-wheat buns
- ¼ cup store-bought tzatziki sauce
- 1 tomato, cut into slices
- 4 thin red onion slices
- ½ cup shredded lettuce

Directions:
1. Preheat the toaster oven to 350°F on CONVECTION BROIL for 5 minutes.
2. In a large bowl, mix the lamb, egg, parsley, mint, garlic, salt, and pepper. Form the mixture into 4 patties.
3. Place the air-fryer basket in the baking tray and place the burger patties in the basket. Lightly spray the patties with the oil on both sides.
4. In position 2, broil for 15 minutes, turning halfway through.
5. Serve on the buns topped with tzatziki sauce, tomato, onion, and lettuce.

Perfect Pork Chops

Servings: 3
Cooking Time: 10 Minutes
Ingredients:
- ¾ teaspoon Mild paprika
- ¾ teaspoon Dried thyme
- ¾ teaspoon Onion powder
- ¼ teaspoon Garlic powder
- ¼ teaspoon Table salt
- ¼ teaspoon Ground black pepper
- 3 6-ounce boneless center-cut pork loin chops
- Vegetable oil spray

Directions:
1. Preheat the toaster oven to 400°F.
2. Mix the paprika, thyme, onion powder, garlic powder, salt, and pepper in a small bowl until well combined. Massage this mixture into both sides of the chops. Generously coat both sides of the chops with vegetable oil spray.
3. When the machine is at temperature, set the chops in the air fryer oven with as much air space between them as possible. Air-fry undisturbed for 10 minutes, or until an instant-read meat thermometer inserted into the thickest part of a chop registers 145°F.
4. Use kitchen tongs to transfer the chops to a cutting board or serving plates. Cool for 5 minutes before serving.

Calf's Liver

Servings: 4
Cooking Time: 5 Minutes
Ingredients:
- 1 pound sliced calf's liver
- salt and pepper
- 2 eggs
- 2 tablespoons milk
- ½ cup whole wheat flour
- 1½ cups panko breadcrumbs
- ½ cup plain breadcrumbs
- ½ teaspoon salt
- ¼ teaspoon pepper
- oil for misting or cooking spray

Directions:
1. Cut liver slices crosswise into strips about ½-inch wide. Sprinkle with salt and pepper to taste.
2. Beat together egg and milk in a shallow dish.
3. Place wheat flour in a second shallow dish.
4. In a third shallow dish, mix together panko, plain breadcrumbs, ½ teaspoon salt, and ¼ teaspoon pepper.
5. Preheat the toaster oven to 390°F.
6. Dip liver strips in flour, egg wash, and then breadcrumbs, pressing in coating slightly to make crumbs stick.
7. Cooking half the liver at a time, place strips in air fryer oven in a single layer, close but not touching. Air-fry at 390°F for 5 minutes or until done to your preference.

8. Repeat step 7 to cook remaining liver.

Meatloaf With Tangy Tomato Glaze

Servings: 6
Cooking Time: 50 Minutes
Ingredients:
- 1 pound ground beef
- ½ pound ground pork
- ½ pound ground veal (or turkey)
- 1 medium onion, diced
- 1 small clove of garlic, minced
- 2 egg yolks, lightly beaten
- ½ cup tomato ketchup
- 1 tablespoon Worcestershire sauce
- ½ cup plain breadcrumbs
- 2 teaspoons salt
- freshly ground black pepper
- ½ cup chopped fresh parsley, plus more for garnish
- 6 tablespoons ketchup
- 1 tablespoon balsamic vinegar
- 2 tablespoons brown sugar

Directions:
1. Combine the meats, onion, garlic, egg yolks, ketchup, Worcestershire sauce, breadcrumbs, salt, pepper and fresh parsley in a large bowl and mix well.
2. Preheat the toaster oven to 350°F and pour a little water into the bottom of the air fryer oven. (This will help prevent the grease that drips into the bottom drawer from burning and smoking.)
3. Transfer the meatloaf mixture to the air fryer oven, packing it down gently. Run a spatula around the meatloaf to create a space about ½-inch wide between the meat and the side of the air fryer oven.
4. Air-fry at 350°F for 20 minutes. Carefully invert the meatloaf onto a plate (remember to remove the pan from the air fryer oven so you don't pour all the grease out) and slide it back into the air fryer oven to turn it over. Re-shape the meatloaf with a spatula if necessary. Air-fry for another 20 minutes at 350°F.
5. Combine the ketchup, balsamic vinegar and brown sugar in a bowl and spread the mixture over the meatloaf. Air-fry for another 10 minutes, until an instant read thermometer inserted into the center of the meatloaf registers 160°F.
6. Allow the meatloaf to rest for a few more minutes and then transfer it to a serving platter using a spatula. Slice the meatloaf, sprinkle a little chopped parsley on top if desired, and serve.

Spanish Pork Skewers

Servings: 4
Cooking Time: 16 Minutes
Ingredients:
- 1 pound pork tenderloin, cut into ¾- to 1-inch cubes
- 2 tablespoons olive oil
- 1 teaspoon ground cumin
- ½ teaspoon smoked paprika
- ½ teaspoon dried thyme leaves
- ½ teaspoon kosher salt, plus more for seasoning
- ⅛ teaspoon red pepper flakes
- 2 cloves garlic, minced
- 1 red bell pepper, cut into ¾- to 1-inch squares
- 1 small red onion, cut into ¾- to 1-inch wedges
- Freshly ground black pepper
- Nonstick cooking spray
- 2 tablespoons unsalted butter
- 1 tablespoon sherry or balsamic vinegar
- 1 teaspoon packed dark brown sugar

Directions:
1. Place the pork cubes in a medium bowl. Drizzle 1 tablespoon of oil over the pork. Stir the cumin, paprika, thyme, ½ teaspoon salt, the pepper flakes, and garlic in a small bowl. Sprinkle the seasonings over the pork. Stir to coat the pork evenly. Cover and refrigerate for at least 4 hours or up to overnight.
2. Place the bell pepper and onion pieces in a medium bowl. Drizzle with the remaining tablespoon olive oil and season with salt and pepper. Toss to coat evenly.
3. Alternately thread the pork and vegetables onto skewers. Spray a 12 x 12-inch baking pan with nonstick cooking spray. Place the filled skewers on the prepared pan. Place the pan in the toaster oven, positioning the skewers about 3 to 4 inches below the heating element. (Depending on your oven, you may need to set the rack to the middle position.)
4. Set the toaster oven on broil. Broil for 10 minutes. Turn the skewers. Broil for an additional 5 minutes, or until the vegetables are tender and a meat thermometer registers 145°F. Do not overcook.
5. Meanwhile, combine the butter, vinegar, and brown sugar in a small, glass, microwave-safe bowl. Season with salt and pepper. Microwave on High (100 percent) power for 45 seconds or until the butter melts and the mixture begins to bubble. Stir to dissolve the sugar.
6. Lightly brush the vinegar mixture over the skewers. Broil for 1 minute or until the skewers are browned.

Italian Sausage & Peppers

Servings: 6
Cooking Time: 25 Minutes
Ingredients:
- 1 6-ounce can tomato paste
- ⅔ cup water
- 1 8-ounce can tomato sauce
- 1 teaspoon dried parsley flakes
- ½ teaspoon garlic powder
- ⅛ teaspoon oregano
- ½ pound mild Italian bulk sausage
- 1 tablespoon extra virgin olive oil

- ½ large onion, cut in 1-inch chunks
- 4 ounces fresh mushrooms, sliced
- 1 large green bell pepper, cut in 1-inch chunks
- 8 ounces spaghetti, cooked
- Parmesan cheese for serving

Directions:

1. In a large saucepan or skillet, stir together the tomato paste, water, tomato sauce, parsley, garlic, and oregano. Heat on stovetop over very low heat while preparing meat and vegetables.

2. Break sausage into small chunks, about ½-inch pieces. Place in air fryer oven baking pan.

3. Air-fry at 390°F for 5 minutes. Stir. Cook 7 minutes longer or until sausage is well done. Remove from pan, drain on paper towels, and add to the sauce mixture.

4. If any sausage grease remains in baking pan, pour it off or use paper towels to soak it up. (Be careful handling that hot pan!)

5. Place olive oil, onions, and mushrooms in pan and stir. Air-fry for 5 minutes or just until tender. Using a slotted spoon, transfer onions and mushrooms from baking pan into the sauce and sausage mixture.

6. Place bell pepper chunks in air fryer oven baking pan and air-fry for 8 minutes or until tender. When done, stir into sauce with sausage and other vegetables.

7. Serve over cooked spaghetti with plenty of Parmesan cheese.

Indian Fry Bread Tacos

Servings: 4

Cooking Time: 20 Minutes

Ingredients:

- 1 cup all-purpose flour
- 1½ teaspoons salt, divided
- 1½ teaspoons baking powder
- ¼ cup milk
- ¼ cup warm water
- ½ pound lean ground beef
- One 14.5-ounce can pinto beans, drained and rinsed
- 1 tablespoon taco seasoning
- ½ cup shredded cheddar cheese
- 2 cups shredded lettuce
- ¼ cup black olives, chopped
- 1 Roma tomato, diced
- 1 avocado, diced
- 1 lime

Directions:

1. In a large bowl, whisk together the flour, 1 teaspoon of the salt, and baking powder. Make a well in the center and add in the milk and water. Form a ball and gently knead the dough four times. Cover the bowl with a damp towel, and set aside.

2. Preheat the toaster oven to 380°F.

3. In a medium bowl, mix together the ground beef, beans, and taco seasoning. Crumble the meat mixture into the air fryer oven and air-fry for 5 minutes; toss the meat and cook an additional 2 to 3 minutes, or until cooked fully. Place the cooked meat in a bowl for taco assembly; season with the remaining ½ teaspoon salt as desired.

4. On a floured surface, place the dough. Cut the dough into 4 equal parts. Using a rolling pin, roll out each piece of dough to 5 inches in diameter. Spray the dough with cooking spray and place in the air fryer oven, working in batches as needed. Air-fry for 3 minutes, flip over, spray with cooking spray, and air-fry for an additional 1 to 3 minutes, until golden and puffy.

5. To assemble, place the fry breads on a serving platter. Equally divide the meat and bean mixture on top of the fry bread. Divide the cheese, lettuce, olives, tomatoes, and avocado among the four tacos. Squeeze lime over the top prior to serving.

Lime And Cumin Lamb Kebabs

Servings: 4

Cooking Time: 16 Minutes

Ingredients:

- 1 pound boneless lean lamb, trimmed and cut into 1 × 1-inch pieces
- 2 plum tomatoes, cut into 2 × 2-inch pieces
- 1 bell pepper, cut into 2 × 2-inch pieces
- 1 small onion, cut into 2 × 2-inch pieces
- Brushing mixture:
- ¼ cup lime juice
- ½ teaspoon soy sauce
- 1 tablespoon honey
- 1½ teaspoon ground cumin

Directions:

1. Skewer alternating pieces of lamb, tomato, pepper, and onion on four 9-inch skewers.

2. Combine the brushing mixture ingredients in a small bowl and brush on the kebabs. Place the skewers on a broiling rack with a pan underneath.

3. BROIL for 8 minutes. Turn the skewers, brush the kebabs with the mixture, and broil for 8 minutes, or until the meat and vegetables are cooked and browned.

Classic Pepperoni Pizza

Servings: 4

Cooking Time: 11 Minutes

Ingredients:

- Oil spray (hand-pumped)
- 1 pound premade pizza dough, or your favorite recipe
- ½ cup store-bought pizza sauce
- ¼ cup grated Parmesan cheese
- ¾ cup shredded mozzarella
- 10 to 12 slices pepperoni
- 2 tablespoons chopped fresh basil

- Pinch red pepper flakes

Directions:

1. Preheat the toaster oven to 425°F on BAKE for 5 minutes.

2. Spray the baking tray with the oil and spread the pizza dough with your fingertips so that it covers the tray. Prick the dough with a fork.

3. In position 2, bake for 8 minutes until the crust is lightly golden.

4. Take the crust out and spread with the pizza sauce, leaving a ½-inch border around the edge. Sprinkle with Parmesan and mozzarella cheeses and arrange the pepperoni on the pizza.

5. Bake for 3 minutes until the cheese is melted and bubbly.

6. Top with the basil and red pepper flakes and serve.

Calzones South Of The Border

Servings: 8
Cooking Time: 8 Minutes

Ingredients:
- Filling
- ¼ pound ground pork sausage
- ½ teaspoon chile powder
- ¼ teaspoon ground cumin
- ⅛ teaspoon garlic powder
- ⅛ teaspoon onion powder
- ⅛ teaspoon oregano
- ½ cup ricotta cheese
- 1 ounce sharp Cheddar cheese, shredded
- 2 ounces Pepper Jack cheese, shredded
- 1 4-ounce can chopped green chiles, drained
- oil for misting or cooking spray
- salsa, sour cream, or guacamole
- Crust
- 2 cups white wheat flour, plus more for kneading and rolling
- 1 package (¼ ounce) RapidRise yeast
- 1 teaspoon salt
- ½ teaspoon chile powder
- ½ teaspoon ground cumin
- 1 cup warm water (115°F to 125°F)
- 2 teaspoons olive oil

Directions:

1. Crumble sausage into air fryer oven baking pan and stir in the filling seasonings: chile powder, cumin, garlic powder, onion powder, and oregano. Air-fry at 390°F for 2 minutes. Stir, breaking apart, and air-fry for 3 to 4 minutes, until well done. Remove and set aside on paper towels to drain.

2. To make dough, combine flour, yeast, salt, chile powder, and cumin. Stir in warm water and oil until soft dough forms. Turn out onto lightly floured board and knead for 3 or 4 minutes. Let dough rest for 10 minutes.

3. Place the three cheeses in a medium bowl. Add cooked sausage and chiles and stir until well mixed.

4. Cut dough into 8 pieces.

5. Working with 4 pieces of the dough, press each into a circle about 5 inches in diameter. Top each dough circle with 2 heaping tablespoons of filling. Fold over into a half-moon shape and press edges together. Seal edges firmly to prevent leakage. Spray both sides with oil or cooking spray.

6. Place 4 calzones in air fryer oven and air-fry at 360°F for 5 minutes. Mist with oil or spray and air-fry for 3 minutes, until crust is done and nicely browned.

7. While the first batch is cooking, press out the remaining dough, fill, and shape into calzones.

8. Spray both sides with oil or cooking spray and air-fry for 5 minutes. If needed, mist with oil and continue cooking for 3 minutes longer. This second batch will cook a little faster than the first because your air fryer oven is already hot.

9. Serve plain or with salsa, sour cream, or guacamole.

Pesto Pork Chops

Servings: 2
Cooking Time: 15 Minutes

Ingredients:
- 2 (6-ounce) boneless pork loin chops
- 2 tablespoons basil pesto

Directions:

1. Preheat the toaster oven to 375°F on AIR FRY for 5 minutes.

2. Rub the pork chops all over with the pesto and set aside for 15 minutes.

3. Place the air-fryer basket in the baking tray and arrange the pork in the basket with no overlap.

4. In position 2, air fry for 15 minutes, turning halfway through, until the chops are lightly browned and have an internal temperature of 145°F.

5. Let the meat rest for 10 minutes and serve.

Seasoned Boneless Pork Sirloin Chops

Servings: 2
Cooking Time: 16 Minutes

Ingredients:
- Seasoning mixture:
- ½ teaspoon ground cumin
- ¼ teaspoon turmeric
- Pinch of ground cardamom
- Pinch of grated nutmeg
- 1 teaspoon vegetable oil
- 1 teaspoon Pickapeppa sauce
- 2½- to ¾-pound boneless lean pork sirloin chops

Directions:

1. Combine the seasoning mixture ingredients in a small bowl and brush on both sides of the chops. Place the chops on the broiling rack with a pan underneath.

2. BROIL 8 minutes, remove the chops, turn, and brush with the mixture. Broil again for 8 minutes, or until the chops are done to your preference.

Stuffed Bell Peppers

Servings: 4
Cooking Time: 10 Minutes
Ingredients:
- ¼ pound lean ground pork
- ¾ pound lean ground beef
- ¼ cup onion, minced
- 1 15-ounce can Red Gold crushed tomatoes
- 1 teaspoon Worcestershire sauce
- 1 teaspoon barbeque seasoning
- 1 teaspoon honey
- ½ teaspoon dried basil
- ½ cup cooked brown rice
- ½ teaspoon garlic powder
- ½ teaspoon oregano
- ½ teaspoon salt
- 2 small bell peppers

Directions:
1. Place pork, beef, and onion in air fryer oven baking pan and air-fry at 360°F for 5 minutes.
2. Stir to break apart chunks and cook 3 more minutes. Continue cooking and stirring in 2-minute intervals until meat is well done. Remove from pan and drain.
3. In a small saucepan, combine the tomatoes, Worcestershire, barbeque seasoning, honey, and basil. Stir well to mix in honey and seasonings.
4. In a large bowl, combine the cooked meat mixture, rice, garlic powder, oregano, and salt. Add ¼ cup of the seasoned crushed tomatoes. Stir until well mixed.
5. Cut peppers in half and remove stems and seeds.
6. Stuff each pepper half with one fourth of the meat mixture.
7. Place the peppers in air fryer oven and air-fry for 10 minutes, until peppers are crisp tender.
8. Heat remaining tomato sauce. Serve peppers with warm sauce spooned over top.

Chinese Pork And Vegetable Non-stir-fry

Servings: 4
Cooking Time: 30 Minutes
Ingredients:
- Seasoning sauce:
- 1 tablespoon soy sauce
- ¼ cup dry white wine
- 1 tablespoon sesame oil
- 1 tablespoon vegetable oil
- 1 teaspoon Chinese five-spice powder
- 2 6-ounce lean boneless pork chops cut into ¼ × 2-inch strips

- 1 1-pound package frozen vegetable mix or 2 cups sliced assorted fresh vegetables: broccoli, carrots, cauliflower, bell pepper, and the like
- 1 4-ounce can mushroom pieces, drained, or ½ cup cleaned and sliced fresh mushrooms
- 2 tablespoons sesame seeds
- 2 tablespoons minced fresh garlic

Directions:
1. Whisk together the seasoning sauce ingredients in a small bowl. Set aside.
2. Combine the pork, vegetables, mushrooms, sesame seeds, and garlic in an oiled or nonstick 8½ × 8½ × 2-inch square baking (cake) pan. Add the seasoning sauce ingredients and toss to coat the pork, vegetables, and mushrooms well.
3. BROIL for 30 minutes, turning with tongs every 8 minutes, until the vegetables and meat are well cooked and lightly browned.

Crispy Lamb Shoulder Chops

Servings: 3
Cooking Time: 28 Minutes
Ingredients:
- ¾ cup All-purpose flour or gluten-free all-purpose flour
- 2 teaspoons Mild paprika
- 2 teaspoons Table salt
- 1½ teaspoons Garlic powder
- 1½ teaspoons Dried sage leaves
- 3 6-ounce bone-in lamb shoulder chops, any excess fat trimmed
- Olive oil spray

Directions:
1. Whisk the flour, paprika, salt, garlic powder, and sage in a large bowl until the mixture is of a uniform color. Add the chops and toss well to coat. Transfer them to a cutting board.
2. Preheat the toaster oven to 375°F .
3. When the machine is at temperature, again dredge the chops one by one in the flour mixture. Lightly coat both sides of each chop with olive oil spray before putting it in the air fryer oven. Continue on with the remaining chop(s), leaving air space between them in the air fryer oven.
4. Air-fry, turning once, for 25 minutes, or until the chops are well browned and tender when pierced with the point of a paring knife. If the machine is at 360°F, you may need to add up to 3 minutes to the cooking time.
5. Use kitchen tongs to transfer the chops to a wire rack. Cool for 5 minutes before serving.

Beef, Onion, And Pepper Shish Kebab

Servings: 4
Cooking Time: 20 Minutes
Ingredients:
• Marinade:
• 2 tablespoons olive oil
• ½ cup dry red wine
• 1 tablespoon soy sauce
• 1 teaspoon chili powder
• 1 teaspoon Worcestershire sauce
• 1 teaspoon garlic powder
• 1 teaspoon spicy brown mustard
• 1 teaspoon brown sugar
• 8 onion quarters, approximately 2 × 2-inch pieces
• 8 bell pepper quarters, 2 × 2-inch pieces
• 1 pound lean boneless beef (sirloin, round steak, London broil), cut into 8 2-inch cubes
• 4 8-inch metal or wooden (bamboo) skewers
Directions:
1. Combine the marinade ingredients in a large bowl. Add the onion, peppers, and beef. Refrigerate, covered, for at least 1 hour or
2. Skewer alternating beef, pepper, and onion pieces. Brush with the marinade mixture and place the skewers on a broiling rack with the pan underneath.
3. BROIL for 5 minutes, remove the pan with the skewers from the oven, turn the skewers, brush again, then broil for another 5 minutes. Repeat turning and brushing every 5 minutes, until the peppers and onions are well cooked and browned to your preference.

Mustard-herb Lamb Chops

Servings: 2
Cooking Time: 15 Minutes
Ingredients:
• 2 tablespoons Dijon mustard
• 1 teaspoon minced garlic
• ¼ cup bread crumbs
• 1 teaspoon dried Italian herbs
• Zest of 1 lemon
• 4 lamb loin chops (about 1 pound), room temperature
• Sea salt, for seasoning
• Freshly ground black pepper, for seasoning
• Oil spray (hand-pumped)
Directions:
1. Preheat the toaster oven to 425°F on CONVECTION BAKE for 5 minutes.
2. Line the baking tray with parchment or aluminum foil.
3. In a small bowl, stir the mustard and garlic until blended.
4. In another small bowl, stir the bread crumbs, herbs, and lemon zest until mixed.
5. Lightly season the lamb chops on both sides with salt and pepper. Brush the mustard mixture over a chop and dredge it in the bread crumb mixture to lightly bread the lamb. Set the lamb on the baking tray and repeat with the other chops.
6. Spray the chops lightly with the oil, and in position 2, bake for 15 minutes until browned and the internal temperature is 130°F for medium-rare.
7. Rest the lamb for 5 minutes, then serve.

Stuffed Pork Chops

Servings: 4
Cooking Time: 12 Minutes
Ingredients:
• 4 boneless pork chops
• ½ teaspoon salt
• ½ teaspoon black pepper
• ¼ teaspoon paprika
• 1 cup frozen spinach, defrosted and squeezed dry
• 2 cloves garlic, minced
• 2 ounces cream cheese
• ¼ cup grated Parmesan cheese
• 1 tablespoon extra-virgin olive oil
Directions:
1. Pat the pork chops with a paper towel. Make a slit in the side of each pork chop to create a pouch.
2. Season the pork chops with the salt, pepper, and paprika.
3. In a small bowl, mix together the spinach, garlic, cream cheese, and Parmesan cheese.
4. Divide the mixture into fourths and stuff the pork chop pouches. Secure the pouches with toothpicks.
5. Preheat the toaster oven to 400°F.
6. Place the stuffed pork chops in the air fryer oven and spray liberally with cooking spray. Air-fry for 6 minutes, flip and coat with more cooking spray, and cook another 6 minutes. Check to make sure the meat is cooked to an internal temperature of 145°F. Cook the pork chops in batches, as needed.

Red Curry Flank Steak

Servings: 4
Cooking Time: 18 Minutes
Ingredients:
• 3 tablespoons red curry paste
• ¼ cup olive oil
• 2 teaspoons grated fresh ginger
• 2 tablespoons soy sauce
• 2 tablespoons rice wine vinegar
• 3 scallions, minced
• 1½ pounds flank steak
• fresh cilantro (or parsley) leaves
Directions:
1. Mix the red curry paste, olive oil, ginger, soy sauce, rice vinegar and scallions together in a bowl. Place the flank

steak in a shallow glass dish and pour half the marinade over the steak. Pierce the steak several times with a fork or meat tenderizer to let the marinade penetrate the meat. Turn the steak over, pour the remaining marinade over the top and pierce the steak several times again. Cover and marinate the steak in the refrigerator for 6 to 8 hours.

2. When you are ready to cook, remove the steak from the refrigerator and let it sit at room temperature for 30 minutes.

3. Preheat the toaster oven to 400°F.

4. Cut the flank steak in half so that it fits more easily into the air fryer oven and transfer both pieces to the air fryer oven. Pour the marinade over the steak. Air-fry for 18 minutes, depending on your preferred degree of doneness of the steak (12 minutes = medium rare). Flip the steak over halfway through the cooking time.

5. When your desired degree of doneness has been reached, remove the steak to a cutting board and let it rest for 5 minutes before slicing. Thinly slice the flank steak against the grain of the meat. Transfer the slices to a serving platter, pour any juice from the bottom of the air fryer oven over the sliced flank steak and sprinkle the fresh cilantro on top.

Pork Taco Gorditas

Servings: 4
Cooking Time: 21 Minutes
Ingredients:
- 1 pound lean ground pork
- 2 tablespoons chili powder
- 2 tablespoons ground cumin
- 1 teaspoon dried oregano
- 2 teaspoons paprika
- 1 teaspoon garlic powder
- ½ cup water
- 1 (15-ounce) can pinto beans, drained and rinsed
- ½ cup taco sauce
- salt and freshly ground black pepper
- 2 cups grated Cheddar cheese
- 5 (12-inch) flour tortillas
- 4 (8-inch) crispy corn tortilla shells
- 4 cups shredded lettuce
- 1 tomato, diced
- ⅓ cup sliced black olives
- sour cream, for serving
- tomato salsa, for serving

Directions:
1. Preheat the toaster oven to 400°F.

2. Place the ground pork in the air fryer oven and air-fry at 400°F for 10 minutes, stirring a few times during the cooking process to gently break up the meat. Combine the chili powder, cumin, oregano, paprika, garlic powder and water in a small bowl. Stir the spice mixture into the browned pork. Stir in the beans and taco sauce and air-fry for an additional minute. Transfer the pork mixture to a bowl. Season to taste with salt and freshly ground black pepper.

3. Sprinkle ½ cup of the shredded cheese in the center of four of the flour tortillas, making sure to leave a 2-inch border around the edge free of cheese and filling. Divide the pork mixture among the four tortillas, placing it on top of the cheese. Place a crunchy corn tortilla on top of the pork and top with shredded lettuce, diced tomatoes, and black olives. Cut the remaining flour tortilla into 4 quarters. These quarters of tortilla will serve as the bottom of the gordita. Place one quarter tortilla on top of each gordita and fold the edges of the bottom flour tortilla up over the sides, enclosing the filling. While holding the seams down, brush the bottom of the gordita with olive oil and place the seam side down on the countertop while you finish the remaining three gorditas.

4. Preheat the toaster oven to 380°F.

5. Air-fry one gordita at a time. Transfer the gordita carefully to the air fryer oven, seam side down. Brush or spray the top tortilla with oil and air-fry for 5 minutes. Carefully turn the gordita over and air-fry for an additional 5 minutes, until both sides are browned. When finished air frying all four gorditas, layer them back into the air fryer oven for an additional minute to make sure they are all warm before serving with sour cream and salsa.

Beef Al Carbon (street Taco Meat)

Servings: 6
Cooking Time: 8 Minutes
Ingredients:
- 1½ pounds sirloin steak, cut into ½-inch cubes
- ¾ cup lime juice
- ½ cup extra-virgin olive oil
- 1 teaspoon ground cumin
- 2 teaspoons garlic powder
- 1 teaspoon salt

Directions:
1. In a large bowl, toss together the steak, lime juice, olive oil, cumin, garlic powder, and salt. Allow the meat to marinate for 30 minutes. Drain off all the marinade and pat the meat dry with paper towels.

2. Preheat the toaster oven to 400°F.

3. Place the meat in the air fryer oven and spray with cooking spray. Cook the meat for 5 minutes, toss the meat, and continue cooking another 3 minutes, until slightly crispy.

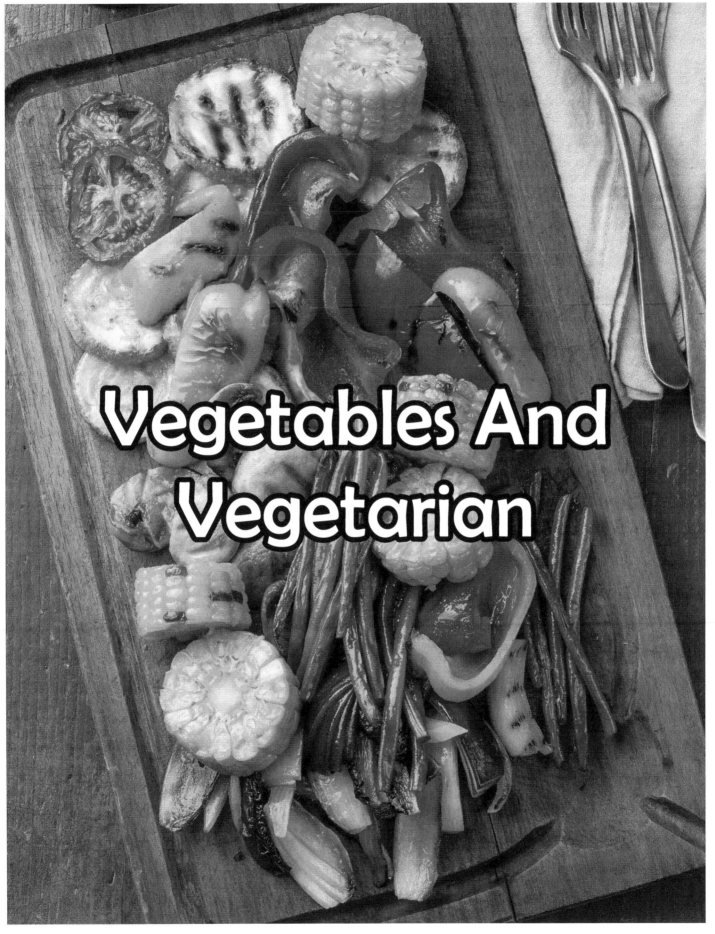

Vegetables And Vegetarian

Vegetables And Vegetarian

Green Beans

Servings: 4
Cooking Time: 12 Minutes
Ingredients:
- 1 pound fresh green beans
- 2 tablespoons Italian salad dressing
- salt and pepper

Directions:
1. Wash beans and snap off stem ends.
2. In a large bowl, toss beans with Italian dressing.
3. Air-fry at 330°F for 5 minutes. Stir and cook 5 minutes longer. If needed, continue cooking for 2 minutes, until as tender as you like. Beans should shrivel slightly and brown in places.
4. Sprinkle with salt and pepper to taste.

Baked Mac And Cheese

Servings: 4
Cooking Time: 45 Minutes
Ingredients:
- Oil spray (hand-pumped)
- 1½ cups whole milk, room temperature
- ½ cup heavy (whipping) cream, room temperature
- 1 cup shredded cheddar cheese
- 4 ounces cream cheese, room temperature
- ½ teaspoon dry mustard
- ⅛ teaspoon sea salt
- ⅛ teaspoon freshly ground black pepper
- 1¼ cups dried elbow macaroni
- ¼ cup bread crumbs
- 2 tablespoons grated Parmesan cheese
- 1 tablespoon salted butter, melted

Directions:
1. Place the rack in position 1 and preheat the toaster oven to 375°F on CONVECTION BAKE for 5 minutes.
2. Lightly coat an 8-inch-square baking dish with the oil spray.
3. In a large bowl, stir the milk, cream, cheddar, cream cheese, mustard, salt, and pepper until well combined.
4. Transfer the mixture to the baking dish, stir in the macaroni and cover tightly with foil.
5. Bake for 35 minutes.
6. While the macaroni is baking, in a small bowl, stir the bread crumbs, Parmesan, and butter to form coarse crumbs. Set aside.
7. Take the baking dish out of the oven, uncover, stir, and evenly cover with the bread crumb mixture.
8. Bake uncovered for an additional 10 minutes until the pasta is tender, bubbly, and golden brown. Serve.

Roasted Eggplant Halves With Herbed Ricotta

Servings: 3
Cooking Time: 20 Minutes
Ingredients:
- 3 5- to 6-ounce small eggplants, stemmed
- Olive oil spray
- ¼ teaspoon Table salt
- ¼ teaspoon Ground black pepper
- ½ cup Regular or low-fat ricotta
- 1½ tablespoons Minced fresh basil leaves
- 1¼ teaspoons Minced fresh oregano leaves
- Honey

Directions:
1. Preheat the toaster oven to 325°F (or 330°F, if that's the closest setting).
2. Cut the eggplants in half lengthwise. Set them cut side up on your work surface. Using the tip of a paring knife, make a series of slits about three-quarters down into the flesh of each eggplant half; work at a 45-degree angle to the (former) stem across the vegetable and make the slits about ½ inch apart. Make a second set of equidistant slits at a 90-degree angle to the first slits, thus creating a crosshatch pattern in the vegetable.
3. Generously coat the cut sides of the eggplants with olive oil spray. Sprinkle the salt and pepper over the cut surfaces.
4. Set the eggplant halves cut side up in the air fryer oven with as much air space between them as possible. Air-fry undisturbed for 20 minutes, or until soft and golden.
5. Use kitchen tongs to gently transfer the eggplant halves to serving plates or a platter. Cool for 5 minutes.
6. Whisk the ricotta, basil, and oregano in a small bowl until well combined. Top the eggplant halves with this mixture. Drizzle the halves with honey to taste before serving warm.

Sweet Potato Curly Fries

Servings: 4
Cooking Time: 10 Minutes
Ingredients:
- 2 medium sweet potatoes, washed
- 2 tablespoons avocado oil
- ¾ teaspoon salt, divided
- 1 medium avocado
- ½ teaspoon garlic powder
- ½ teaspoon paprika
- ¼ teaspoon black pepper
- ½ juice lime
- 3 tablespoons fresh cilantro

Directions:
1. Preheat the toaster oven to 400°F.
2. Using a spiralizer, create curly spirals with the sweet potatoes. Keep the pieces about 1½ inches long. Continue until all the potatoes arc uscd.
3. In a large bowl, toss the curly sweet potatoes with the avocado oil and ½ teaspoon of the salt.
4. Place the potatoes in the air fryer oven and air-fry for 5 minutes; cook another 5 minutes.
5. While cooking, add the avocado, garlic, paprika, pepper, the remaining ¼ teaspoon of salt, lime juice, and cilantro to a blender and process until smooth. Set aside.
6. When cooking completes, remove the fries and serve warm with the lime avocado sauce.

Marjoram New Potatoes

Servings: 2
Cooking Time: 40 Minutes
Ingredients:
- 6 small new red potatoes, scrubbed and halved
- 1 tablespoon olive oil
- 1 tablespoon balsamic vinegar
- 1 tablespoon fresh marjoram leaves, chopped, or 1 teaspoon dried marjoram
- Salt and freshly ground black pepper to taste

Directions:
1. Preheat the toaster oven to 400° F.
2. Combine all the ingredients in a medium bowl and mix well to coat the potatoes.
3. Place in an oiled or nonstick 8½ × 8½ × 2-inch square baking (cake) pan.
4. BAKE, covered, for 30 minutes, or until the potatoes are tender.
5. BROIL 10 minutes to brown to your preference. Serve with balsamic vinegar in a small pitcher to drizzle over.

Parmesan Garlic Fries

Servings: 4
Cooking Time: 20 Minutes
Ingredients:
- 2 medium Yukon gold potatoes, washed
- 1 tablespoon extra-virgin olive oil
- 1 garlic clove, minced
- 2 tablespoons finely grated parmesan cheese
- ¼ teaspoon black pepper
- ¼ teaspoon salt
- 1 tablespoon freshly chopped parsley

Directions:
1. Preheat the toaster oven to 400°F.
2. Slice the potatoes into long strips about ¼-inch thick. In a large bowl, toss the potatoes with the olive oil, garlic, cheese, pepper, and salt.
3. Place the fries into the air fryer oven and air-fry for 8 minutes.
4. Remove and serve warm.

Moroccan Cauliflower

Servings: 6
Cooking Time: 15 Minutes
Ingredients:
- 1 tablespoon curry powder
- 2 teaspoons smoky paprika
- ½ teaspoon ground cumin
- ½ teaspoon salt
- 1 head cauliflower, cut into bite-size pieces
- ¼ cup red wine vinegar
- 2 tablespoons extra-virgin olive oil
- 2 tablespoons chopped parsley

Directions:
1. Preheat the toaster oven to 370°F.
2. In a large bowl, mix the curry powder, paprika, cumin, and salt. Add the cauliflower and stir to coat. Pour the red wine vinegar over the top and continue stirring.
3. Place the cauliflower into the air fryer oven; drizzle olive oil over the top.
4. Cook the cauliflower for 5 minutes, toss, and cook another 5 minutes. Raise the temperature to 400°F and continue cooking for 4 to 6 minutes, or until crispy.

Latkes

Servings: 12
Cooking Time: 13 Minutes

Ingredients:
- 1 russet potato
- ¼ onion
- 2 eggs, lightly beaten
- ⅓ cup flour
- ½ teaspoon baking powder
- 1 teaspoon salt
- freshly ground black pepper
- canola or vegetable oil, in a spray bottle
- chopped chives, for garnish
- apple sauce
- sour cream

Directions:
1. Shred the potato and onion with a coarse box grater or a food processor with the shredding blade. Place the shredded vegetables into a colander or mesh strainer and squeeze or press down firmly to remove the excess water.
2. Transfer the onion and potato to a large bowl and add the eggs, flour, baking powder, salt and black pepper. Mix to combine and then shape the mixture into patties, about ¼-cup of mixture each. Brush or spray both sides of the latkes with oil.
3. Preheat the toaster oven to 400°F.
4. Air-fry the latkes in batches. Transfer one layer of the latkes to the air fryer oven and air-fry at 400°F for 12 to 13 minutes, flipping them over halfway through the cooking time. Transfer the finished latkes to a platter and cover with aluminum foil, or place them in a warm oven to keep warm.
5. Garnish the latkes with chopped chives and serve with sour cream and applesauce.

Ranch Potatoes

Servings: 2
Cooking Time: 50 Minutes

Ingredients:
- 2 medium russet potatoes, scrubbed and cut lengthwise into ¼-inch strips
- 1 medium onion, chopped
- 2 tablespoons vegetable oil
- 2 tablespoons barbecue sauce
- ¼ teaspoon hot sauce
- Salt and freshly ground black pepper

Directions:
1. Preheat the toaster oven to 400° F.
2. Combine all the ingredients in a medium bowl, mixing well and adjusting the seasonings to taste.
3. Place equal portions of the potatoes on two 12 × 12-inch squares of heavy-duty aluminum foil. Fold up the edges of the foil to form a sealed packet and place on the oven rack.
4. BAKE for 40 minutes, or until the potatoes are tender.

Carefully open the packet and fold back the foil.
5. BROIL 10 minutes, or until the potatoes are browned.

Asparagus And Cherry Tomato Quiche

Servings: 4
Cooking Time: 50 Minutes

Ingredients:
- 6 asparagus spears, woody ends removed, cut into 1-inch pieces
- 1 premade unbaked pie crust
- 5 large eggs
- ½ cup half-and-half
- ¾ cup shredded Swiss cheese, divided
- Sea salt, for seasoning
- Freshly ground black pepper, for seasoning
- 10 cherry tomatoes, quartered
- 1 scallion, both white and green parts, finely chopped

Directions:
1. Place the rack in position 1 and preheat oven to 350°F on BAKE for 5 minutes.
2. Place a small saucepan three-quarters filled with water on high heat and bring to a boil. Blanch the asparagus until bright green, about 1 minute. Drain and set aside.
3. Line an 8-inch-round pie dish with the pie crust, then trim and flute the edges.
4. In a small bowl, beat the eggs, half-and-half, and ½ cup of the cheese until well blended; season with salt and pepper.
5. Arrange the asparagus, tomatoes, and scallion in the pie crust. Pour in the egg mixture and top with the remaining ¼ cup of cheese.
6. Bake for 45 to 50 minutes until the quiche is puffed and lightly browned, and a knife inserted in the center comes out clean.
7. Serve warm or cold.

Pecan Parmesan Cauliflower

Servings: 4
Cooking Time: 35 Minutes

Ingredients:
- 2½ cups (frozen thawed or fresh) thinly sliced cauliflower florets
- Salt and freshly ground black pepper
- 3 tablespoons freshly grated Parmesan cheese
- ½ cup ground pecans

Directions:
1. Preheat the toaster oven to 400° F.
2. Combine the florets and oil in a 1-quart 8½ × 8½ × 4-inch ovenproof baking dish, tossing to coat well. Season to taste with salt and pepper. Cover the dish with aluminum foil.
3. BAKE for 25 minutes, or until tender. Uncover and sprinkle with the cheese and pecans.
4. BROIL for 10 minutes, or until lightly browned.

Roasted Ratatouille Vegetables

Servings: 15
Cooking Time: 2 Minutes
Ingredients:
- 1 baby or Japanese eggplant, cut into 1½-inch cubes
- 1 red pepper, cut into 1-inch chunks
- 1 yellow pepper, cut into 1-inch chunks
- 1 zucchini, cut into 1-inch chunks
- 1 clove garlic, minced
- ½ teaspoon dried basil
- 1 tablespoon olive oil
- salt and freshly ground black pepper
- ¼ cup sliced sun-dried tomatoes in oil
- 2 tablespoons chopped fresh basil

Directions:
1. Preheat the toaster oven to 400°F.
2. Toss the eggplant, peppers and zucchini with the garlic, dried basil, olive oil, salt and freshly ground black pepper.
3. Air-fry the vegetables at 400°F for 15 minutes.
4. As soon as the vegetables are tender, toss them with the sliced sun-dried tomatoes and fresh basil and serve.

Balsamic Sweet Potatoes

Servings: 4
Cooking Time: 40 Minutes
Ingredients:
- 2 medium sweet potatoes, scrubbed (or peeled) and sliced into 1-inch rounds
- 3 tablespoons olive oil
- 2 tablespoons balsamic vinegar
- 2 teaspoons molasses
- ½ teaspoon garlic powder
- Salt and freshly ground black pepper to taste
- 1 tablespoon grated lemon zest

Directions:
1. Preheat the toaster oven to 400° F.
2. Mix the potatoes, oil, balsamic vinegar, molasses, and garlic powder together in an oiled or nonstick 8½ × 8½ × 2-inch square baking (cake) pan. Cover the pan with aluminum foil.
3. BAKE, covered, for 30 minutes, or until tender. Remove the cover.
4. BROIL for 10 minutes, or until the potatoes are lightly browned. Season to taste with salt and pepper and garnish with the lemon zest.

Fried Okra

Servings: 4
Cooking Time: 8 Minutes
Ingredients:
- 1 pound okra
- 1 large egg
- 1 tablespoon milk
- 1 teaspoon salt, divided
- ½ teaspoon black pepper, divided
- ¼ teaspoon paprika
- ¼ teaspoon thyme
- ½ cup cornmeal
- ½ cup all-purpose flour

Directions:
1. Preheat the toaster oven to 400°F.
2. Cut the okra into ½-inch rounds.
3. In a medium bowl, whisk together the egg, milk, ½ teaspoon of the salt, and ¼ teaspoon of black pepper. Place the okra into the egg mixture and toss until well coated.
4. In a separate bowl, mix together the remaining ½ teaspoon of salt, the remaining ¼ teaspoon of black pepper, the paprika, the thyme, the cornmeal, and the flour. Working in small batches, dredge the egg-coated okra in the cornmeal mixture until all the okra has been breaded.
5. Place a single layer of okra in the air fryer oven and spray with cooking spray. Air-fry for 4 minutes, toss to check for crispness, and cook another 4 minutes. Repeat in batches, as needed.

Roasted Veggie Kebabs

Servings: 4
Cooking Time: 45 Minutes
Ingredients:
- Brushing mixture:
- 3 tablespoons olive oil
- 1 tablespoon soy sauce
- 1 teaspoon garlic powder
- 1 teaspoon ground cumin
- 2 tablespoons balsamic vinegar
- Salt and freshly ground black pepper to taste
- Cauliflower, zucchini, onion, broccoli, bell pepper, mushrooms, celery, cabbage, beets, and the like, cut into approximately 2 × 2-inch pieces

Directions:
1. Preheat the toaster oven to 400° F.
2. Combine the brushing mixture ingredients in a small bowl, mixing well. Set aside.
3. Skewer the vegetable pieces on 4 9-inch metal skewers and place the skewers lengthwise on a broiling rack with a pan underneath.
4. BAKE for 40 minutes, or until the vegetables are tender, brushing with the mixture every 10 minutes.
5. BROIL for 5 minutes, or until lightly browned.

Chilaquiles

Servings: 4

Cooking Time: 25 Minutes

Ingredients:
- Oil spray (hand-pumped)
- 1¼ cups store-bought salsa
- 1 (15-ounce) can low-sodium navy or black beans, drained and rinsed
- ½ cup corn kernels
- ¼ cup chicken broth
- ¼ sweet onion, chopped
- ½ teaspoon minced garlic
- 25 tortilla chips, broken up into 2-inch pieces
- 1½ cups queso fresco cheese, crumbled
- 1 avocado, chopped
- 1 scallion, white and green parts, chopped

Directions:
1. Place the rack in position 1 and preheat the toaster oven to 400°F on BAKE for 5 minutes.
2. Lightly coat an 8-inch-square baking dish with oil spray and set aside.
3. In a large bowl, stir the salsa, beans, corn, chicken broth, onion, and garlic until well mixed.
4. Add the tortilla chips and stir to combine. It is okay if the tortilla chips break up a little.
5. Transfer the mixture to the baking dish, top with the cheese, and cover tightly with foil.
6. Bake for 20 minutes until the chips are soft, the mixture is bubbly, and then uncover and bake until the cheese is golden and melted, about 5 minutes.
7. Serve topped with the avocado and scallion.

Crunchy Roasted Potatoes

Servings: 5

Cooking Time: 25 Minutes

Ingredients:
- 2 pounds Small (1- to 1½-inch-diameter) red, white, or purple potatoes
- 2 tablespoons Olive oil
- 2 teaspoons Table salt
- ¾ teaspoon Garlic powder
- ½ teaspoon Ground black pepper

Directions:
1. Preheat the toaster oven to 400°F.
2. Toss the potatoes, oil, salt, garlic powder, and pepper in a large bowl until the spuds are evenly and thoroughly coated.
3. When the machine is at temperature, pour the potatoes into the air fryer oven, spreading them into an even layer (although they may be stacked on top of each other). Air-fry for 25 minutes, tossing twice, until the potatoes are tender but crunchy.
4. Pour the contents of the air fryer oven into a serving

bowl. Cool for 5 minutes before serving.

Stuffed Onions

Servings: 6

Cooking Time: 27 Minutes

Ingredients:
- 6 Small 3½- to 4-ounce yellow or white onions
- Olive oil spray
- 6 ounces Bulk sweet Italian sausage meat (gluten-free, if a concern)
- 9 Cherry tomatoes, chopped
- 3 tablespoons Seasoned Italian-style dried bread crumbs (gluten-free, if a concern)
- 3 tablespoons (about ½ ounce) Finely grated Parmesan cheese

Directions:
1. Preheat the toaster oven to 325°F (or 330°F, if that's the closest setting).
2. Cut just enough off the root ends of the onions so they will stand up on a cutting board when this end is turned down. Carefully peel off just the brown, papery skin. Now cut the top quarter off each and place the onion back on the cutting board with this end facing up. Use a flatware spoon (preferably a serrated grapefruit spoon) or a melon baller to scoop out the "insides" (interior layers) of the onion, leaving enough of the bottom and side walls so that the onion does not collapse. Depending on the thickness of the layers in the onion, this may be one or two of those layers—or even three, if they're very thin.
3. Coat the insides and outsides of the onions with olive oil spray. Set the onion "shells" in the air fryer oven and air-fry for 15 minutes.
4. Meanwhile, make the filling. Set a medium skillet over medium heat for a couple of minutes, then crumble in the sausage meat. Cook, stirring often, until browned, about 4 minutes. Transfer the contents of the skillet to a medium bowl (leave the fat behind in the skillet or add it to the bowl, depending on your cross-trainer regimen). Stir in the tomatoes, bread crumbs, and cheese until well combined.
5. When the onions are ready, use a nonstick-safe spatula to gently transfer them to a cutting board. Increase the air fryer oven's temperature to 350°F .
6. Pack the sausage mixture into the onion shells, gently compacting the filling and mounding it up at the top.
7. When the machine is at temperature, set the onions stuffing side up in the air fryer oven with at least ¼ inch between them. Air-fry for 12 minutes, or until lightly browned and sizzling hot.
8. Use a nonstick-safe spatula, and perhaps a flatware fork for balance, to transfer the onions to a cutting board or serving platter. Cool for 5 minutes before serving.

Potatoes Au Gratin

Servings: 4
Cooking Time: 40 Minutes
Ingredients:
- Mixture:
- ½ cup fat-free half-and-half
- ¼ cup nonfat plain yogurt
- 2 tablespoons margarine
- 2 tablespoons unbleached flour
- 1 teaspoon garlic powder
- ¼ cup shredded low-fat mozzarella cheese
- 2 tablespoons grated Parmesan cheese
- Salt and butcher's pepper to taste
- 2 cups peeled and diced potatoes
- ½ cup chopped onion
- 1 tablespoon fresh or frozen chives
- ¼ teaspoon paprika

Directions:
1. Preheat the toaster oven to 400° F.
2. Process the mixture ingredients in a food processor or blender until smooth. Pour into a 1-quart 8½ × 8½ × 4-inch ovenproof baking dish.
3. Add the potatoes, onion, chives, and paprika and stir to mix well. Cover the dish with aluminum foil.
4. BAKE, covered, for 40 minutes, or until the potatoes and onion are tender.

Glazed Carrots

Servings: 4
Cooking Time: 10 Minutes
Ingredients:
- 2 teaspoons honey
- 1 teaspoon orange juice
- ½ teaspoon grated orange rind
- ⅛ teaspoon ginger
- 1 pound baby carrots
- 2 teaspoons olive oil
- ¼ teaspoon salt

Directions:
1. Combine honey, orange juice, grated rind, and ginger in a small bowl and set aside.
2. Toss the carrots, oil, and salt together to coat well and pour them into the air fryer oven.
3. Air-fry at 390°F for 5 minutes. Stir a little and air-fry for 4 minutes more, until carrots are barely tender.
4. Pour carrots into air fryer oven baking pan.
5. Stir the honey mixture to combine well, pour glaze over carrots, and stir to coat.
6. Air-fry at 360°F for 1 minute or just until heated through.

Home Fries

Servings: 4
Cooking Time: 20 Minutes
Ingredients:
- 3 pounds potatoes, cut into 1-inch cubes
- ½ teaspoon oil
- salt and pepper

Directions:
1. In a large bowl, mix the potatoes and oil thoroughly.
2. Air-fry at 390°F for 10 minutes and redistribute potatoes.
3. Air-fry for an additional 10 minutes, until brown and crisp.
4. Season with salt and pepper to taste.

Yellow Squash With Bell Peppers

Servings: 4
Cooking Time: 50 Minutes
Ingredients:
- Squash mixture:
- 2 cups yellow (summer) squash, thinly sliced
- ⅓ cup dry white wine
- 1 bell pepper, seeded and sliced into thin strips
- 1 6½-ounce jar marinated artichoke hearts, drained and sliced
- 1 tablespoon minced fresh garlic
- 1 5-ounce can diced pimientos, drained
- Salt and freshly ground black pepper to taste
- ¼ cup shredded part-skim mozzarella cheese
- 3 tablespoons Homemade Bread Crumbs
- 2 tablespoons chopped fresh cilantro

Directions:
1. Preheat the toaster oven to 400° F.
2. Combine the squash mixture ingredients in a 1-quart 8½ × 8½ × 4-inch ovenproof baking dish, mixing well. Adjust the seasonings.
3. BAKE, covered, for 40 minutes, or until the vegetables are tender. Uncover and sprinkle with the cheese and bread crumbs.
4. BROIL 10 minutes, or until the top is lightly browned. Garnish with the chopped cilantro before serving.

Five-spice Roasted Sweet Potatoes

Servings: 4
Cooking Time: 12 Minutes

Ingredients:

- ½ teaspoon ground cinnamon
- ¼ teaspoon ground cumin
- ¼ teaspoon paprika
- 1 teaspoon chile powder
- ⅛ teaspoon turmeric
- ½ teaspoon salt (optional)
- freshly ground black pepper
- 2 large sweet potatoes, peeled and cut into ¾-inch cubes (about 3 cups)
- 1 tablespoon olive oil

Directions:

1. In a large bowl, mix together cinnamon, cumin, paprika, chile powder, turmeric, salt, and pepper to taste.
2. Add potatoes and stir well.
3. Drizzle the seasoned potatoes with the olive oil and stir until evenly coated.
4. Place seasoned potatoes in the air fryer oven baking pan or an ovenproof dish that fits inside your air fryer oven.
5. Air-fry for 6 minutes at 390°F, stop, and stir well.
6. Air-fry for an additional 6 minutes.

Roasted Fennel Salad

Servings: 3
Cooking Time: 20 Minutes

Ingredients:

- 3 cups (about ¾ pound) Trimmed fennel, roughly chopped
- 1½ tablespoons Olive oil
- ¼ teaspoon Table salt
- ¼ teaspoon Ground black pepper
- 1½ tablespoons White balsamic vinegar

Directions:

1. Preheat the toaster oven to 400°F.
2. Toss the fennel, olive oil, salt, and pepper in a large bowl until the fennel is well coated in the oil.
3. When the machine is at temperature, pour the fennel into the air fryer oven, spreading it out into as close to one layer as possible. Air-fry for 20 minutes, tossing and rearranging the fennel pieces twice so that any covered or touching parts get exposed to the air currents, until golden at the edges and softened.
4. Pour the fennel into a serving bowl. Add the vinegar while hot. Toss well, then cool a couple of minutes before serving. Or serve at room temperature.

Crispy Brussels Sprouts

Servings: 3
Cooking Time: 12 Minutes

Ingredients:

- 1¼ pounds Medium, 2-inch-in-length Brussels sprouts
- 1½ tablespoons Olive oil
- ¾ teaspoon Table salt

Directions:

1. Preheat the toaster oven to 400°F.
2. Halve each Brussels sprout through the stem end, pulling off and discarding any discolored outer leaves. Put the sprout halves in a large bowl, add the oil and salt, and stir well to coat evenly, until the Brussels sprouts are glistening.
3. When the machine is at temperature, scrape the contents of the bowl into the air fryer oven, gently spreading the Brussels sprout halves into as close to one layer as possible. Air-fry for 12 minutes, gently tossing and rearranging the vegetables twice to get all covered or touching parts exposed to the air currents, until crisp and browned at the edges.
4. Gently pour the contents of the air fryer oven onto a wire rack. Cool for a minute or two before serving.

Grits Again

Servings: 2
Cooking Time: 10 Minutes

Ingredients:

- cooked grits
- plain breadcrumbs
- oil for misting or cooking spray
- honey or maple syrup for serving (optional)

Directions:

1. While grits are still warm, spread them into a square or rectangular baking pan, about ½-inch thick. If your grits are thicker than that, scoop some out into another pan.
2. Chill several hours or overnight, until grits are cold and firm.
3. When ready to cook, pour off any water that has collected in pan and cut grits into 2- to 3-inch squares.
4. Dip grits squares in breadcrumbs and place in air fryer oven in single layer, close but not touching.
5. Air-fry at 390°F for 10 minutes, until heated through and crispy brown on the outside.
6. Serve while hot either plain or with a drizzle of honey or maple syrup.

Panzanella Salad With Crispy Croutons

Servings: 4

Cooking Time: 3 Minutes

Ingredients:
- ½ French baguette, sliced in half lengthwise
- 2 large cloves garlic
- 2 large ripe tomatoes, divided
- 2 small Persian cucumbers, quartered and diced
- ¼ cup Kalamata olives
- 1 tablespoon chopped, fresh oregano or 1 teaspoon dried oregano
- ¼ cup chopped fresh basil
- ¼ cup chopped fresh parsley
- ½ cup sliced red onion
- 2 tablespoons red wine vinegar
- ¼ cup extra-virgin olive oil
- Salt and pepper, to taste

Directions:
1. Preheat the toaster oven to 380°F.
2. Place the baguette into the air fryer oven and toast for 3 to 5 minutes or until lightly golden brown.
3. Remove the bread from air fryer oven and immediately rub 1 raw garlic clove firmly onto the inside portion of each piece of bread, scraping the garlic onto the bread.
4. Slice 1 of the tomatoes in half and rub the cut edge of one half of the tomato onto the toasted bread. Season the rubbed bread with sea salt to taste.
5. Cut the bread into cubes and place in a large bowl. Cube the remaining 1½ tomatoes and add to the bowl. Add the cucumbers, olives, oregano, basil, parsley, and onion; stir to mix. Drizzle the red wine vinegar into the bowl, and stir. Drizzle the olive oil over the top, stir, and adjust the seasonings with salt and pepper.
6. Serve immediately or allow to sit at room temperature up to 1 hour before serving.

Homemade Potato Puffs

Servings: 4

Cooking Time: 15 Minutes

Ingredients:
- 1¾ cups Water
- 4 tablespoons (¼ cup/½ stick) Butter
- 2 cups plus 2 tablespoons Instant mashed potato flakes
- 1½ teaspoons Table salt
- ¾ teaspoon Ground black pepper
- ¼ teaspoon Mild paprika
- ¼ teaspoon Dried thyme
- 1¼ cups Seasoned Italian-style dried bread crumbs (gluten-free, if a concern)
- Olive oil spray

Directions:
1. Heat the water with the butter in a medium saucepan set over medium-low heat just until the butter melts. Do not bring to a boil.
2. Remove the saucepan from the heat and stir in the potato flakes, salt, pepper, paprika, and thyme until smooth. Set aside to cool for 5 minutes.
3. Preheat the toaster oven to 400°F. Spread the bread crumbs on a dinner plate.
4. Scrape up 2 tablespoons of the potato flake mixture and form it into a small, oblong puff, like a little cylinder about 1½ inches long. Gently roll the puff in the bread crumbs until coated on all sides. Set it aside and continue making more, about 12 for the small batch, 18 for the medium batch, or 24 for the large.
5. Coat the potato cylinders with olive oil spray on all sides, then arrange them in the air fryer oven in one layer with some air space between them. Air-fry undisturbed for 15 minutes, or until crisp and brown.
6. Gently dump the contents of the air fryer oven onto a wire rack. Cool for 5 minutes before serving.

Roasted Heirloom Carrots With Orange And Thyme

Servings: 2

Cooking Time: 12 Minutes

Ingredients:
- 10 to 12 heirloom or rainbow carrots (about 1 pound), scrubbed but not peeled
- 1 teaspoon olive oil
- salt and freshly ground black pepper
- 1 tablespoon butter
- 1 teaspoon fresh orange zest
- 1 teaspoon chopped fresh thyme

Directions:
1. Preheat the toaster oven to 400°F.
2. Scrub the carrots and halve them lengthwise. Toss them in the olive oil, season with salt and freshly ground black pepper and transfer to the air fryer oven.
3. Air-fry at 400°F for 12 minutes.
4. As soon as the carrots have finished cooking, add the butter, orange zest and thyme and toss all the ingredients together in the air fryer oven to melt the butter and coat evenly. Serve warm.

Fried Green Tomatoes With Sriracha Mayo

Servings: 4
Cooking Time: 12 Minutes
Ingredients:
- 3 green tomatoes
- salt and freshly ground black pepper
- ⅓ cup all-purpose flour
- 2 eggs
- ½ cup buttermilk
- 1 cup panko breadcrumbs
- 1 cup cornmeal
- olive oil, in a spray bottle
- fresh thyme sprigs or chopped fresh chives
- Sriracha Mayo
- ½ cup mayonnaise
- 1 to 2 tablespoons sriracha hot sauce
- 1 tablespoon milk

Directions:
1. Cut the tomatoes in ¼-inch slices. Pat them dry with a clean kitchen towel and season generously with salt and pepper.
2. Set up a dredging station using three shallow dishes. Place the flour in the first shallow dish, whisk the eggs and buttermilk together in the second dish, and combine the panko breadcrumbs and cornmeal in the third dish.
3. Preheat the toaster oven to 400°F.
4. Dredge the tomato slices in flour to coat on all sides. Then dip them into the egg mixture and finally press them into the breadcrumbs to coat all sides of the tomato.
5. Spray or brush the air-fryer oven with olive oil. Transfer 3 to 4 tomato slices into the air fryer oven and spray the top with olive oil. Air-fry the tomatoes at 400°F for 8 minutes. Flip them over, spray the other side with oil and air-fry for an additional 4 minutes until golden brown.
6. While the tomatoes are cooking, make the sriracha mayo. Combine the mayonnaise, 1 tablespoon of the sriracha hot sauce and milk in a small bowl. Stir well until the mixture is smooth. Add more sriracha sauce to taste.
7. When the tomatoes are done, transfer them to a cooling rack or a platter lined with paper towels so the bottom does not get soggy. Before serving, carefully stack the all the tomatoes into air fryer oven and air-fry at 350°F for 1 to 2 minutes to heat them back up.
8. Serve the fried green tomatoes hot with the sriracha mayo on the side. Season one last time with salt and freshly ground black pepper and garnish with sprigs of fresh thyme or chopped fresh chives.

Baked Stuffed Acorn Squash

Servings: 2
Cooking Time: 25 Minutes
Ingredients:
- Stuffing:
- ¼ cup multigrain bread crumbs
- 1 tablespoon olive oil
- ¼ cup canned or frozen thawed corn
- 2 tablespoons chopped onion
- 1 teaspoon capers
- 1 teaspoon garlic powder
- Salt and freshly ground black pepper
- 1 medium acorn squash, halved and seeds scooped out

Directions:
1. Preheat the toaster oven to 400° F.
2. Combine the stuffing ingredients and season to taste. Fill the squash cavities with the mixture and place in an oiled or nonstick 8½ × 8½ × 2-inch square baking (cake) pan.
3. BAKE for 25 minutes, or until the squash is tender and the stuffing is lightly browned.

Lunch And Dinner

Lunch And Dinner

Oven-baked Rice

Servings: 2
Cooking Time: 40 Minutes
Ingredients:
- ¼ cup regular rice (not parboiled or precooked)
- Seasonings:
- 1 tablespoon olive oil
- 1 teaspoon dried parsley or
- 1 tablespoon chopped fresh parsley
- 1 teaspoon garlic powder or roasted garlic
- Salt and freshly ground black pepper to taste

Directions:
1. Preheat the toaster oven to 400° F.
2. Combine ¼ cups water and the rice in a 1-quart 8½ × 8½ × 4-inch ovenproof baking dish. Stir well to blend. Cover with aluminum foil.
3. BAKE, covered, for 30 minutes, or until the rice is almost cooked. Add the seasonings, fluff with a fork to combine the seasonings well, then let the rice sit, covered, for 10 minutes. Fluff once more before serving.

Yeast Dough For Two Pizzas

Servings: 8
Cooking Time: 20 Minutes
Ingredients:
- ¼ cup tepid water
- 1 cup tepid skim milk
- ½ teaspoon sugar
- 1 1¼-ounce envelope dry yeast
- 2 cups unbleached flour
- 1 tablespoon olive oil

Directions:
1. Preheat the toaster oven to 400° F.
2. Combine the water, milk, and sugar in a bowl. Add the yeast and set aside for 3 to 5 minutes, or until the yeast is dissolved.
3. Stir in the flour gradually, adding just enough to form a ball of the dough.
4. KNEAD on a floured surface until the dough is satiny, and then put the dough in a bowl in a warm place with a damp towel over the top. In 1 hour or when the dough has doubled in bulk, punch it down and divide it in half. Flatten the dough and spread it out to the desired thickness on an oiled or nonstick 9¾-inch-diameter pie pan. Spread with Homemade Pizza Sauce (recipe follows) and add any desired toppings.
5. BAKE for 20 minutes, or until the topping ingredients are cooked and the cheese is melted.

Favorite Baked Ziti

Servings: 4
Cooking Time: 30 Minutes
Ingredients:
- 2 tablespoons olive oil
- 1 small onion, diced
- 3 cloves garlic, minced
- ¼ teaspoon red pepper flakes
- 1 pound lean ground beef
- ½ teaspoon kosher salt
- ¼ cup dry red wine
- 1 (14.5-ounce) can crushed tomatoes
- 1 tablespoon tomato paste
- 16 ounces ziti, uncooked
- Nonstick cooking spray
- ⅓ cup grated Parmesan cheese
- 1 ½ cups shredded mozzarella cheese
- 2 ounces fresh mozzarella cheese, cut into cubes (about ½ cup)

Directions:
1. Heat the olive oil in a large skillet over medium-high heat. Add the onion and cook, stirring frequently, until tender, 3 to 4 minutes. Stir in the garlic and red pepper flakes. Add the ground beef and salt. Cook, breaking up the ground beef, until the meat is brown and cooked through. Drain well, if needed, and return to the skillet.
2. Add the wine and cook for 2 minutes. Add the tomatoes, tomato paste, and ¾ cup water. Reduce the heat and simmer, uncovered, for 20 to 25 minutes, stirring occasionally.
3. Cook the ziti according to the package directions, except reduce the cooking time to 7 minutes. The ziti will be harder than Al Dente, which is what you want. Drain and rinse under cold water. Transfer to a large bowl.
4. Preheat the toaster oven to 425 °F. Spray an 11 x 7 x 2 ½-inch baking dish with nonstick cooking spray. Spoon about 1 cup of the meat sauce into the prepared dish. Add half of the ziti in an even layer. Spoon about half of the remaining sauce over the ziti. Sprinkle with half the Parmesan and all the shredded mozzarella. Add the remaining half of ziti and cover with the remaining sauce. Sprinkle the remaining Parmesan on top.
5. Bake, covered, for 20 minutes. Remove from the oven and add the cubes of fresh mozzarella. Bake, uncovered, for an additional 10 minutes. If desired, turn to broil for a few minutes to make the top crispy and brown.
6. Remove from the oven and let stand for 10 minutes before serving.

Baked Tomato Casserole

Servings: 4
Cooking Time:45 Minutes
Ingredients:
- Casserole mixture:
- 1 medium onion, coarsely chopped
- 3 medium tomatoes, coarsely chopped
- 1 medium green pepper, coarsely chopped
- 2 garlic cloves, minced
- ½ teaspoon crushed oregano
- ½ teaspoon crushed basil
- 1 tablespoon extra virgin olive oil
- 2 tablespoons chopped fresh cilantro
- Salt and freshly ground black pepper
- 3 4 tablespoons grated Parmesan cheese
- ¼ cup multigrain bread crumbs

Directions:
1. Preheat the toaster oven to 400° F.
2. Combine the casserole mixture ingredients in a 1-quart 8½ × 8½ × 4-inch ovenproof baking dish. Adjust the seasonings to taste and cover with aluminum foil.
3. BAKE, covered, for 35 minutes, or until the tomatoes and pepper are tender. Remove from the oven, uncover, and sprinkle with the bread crumbs and Parmesan cheese.
4. BROIL for 10 minutes, or until the topping is lightly browned.

Parmesan Artichoke Pizza

Servings: 6
Cooking Time: 15 Minutes
Ingredients:
- CRUST
- ¾ cup warm water (110°F)
- 1 ½ teaspoons active dry yeast
- ¼ teaspoon sugar
- 1 tablespoon olive oil
- 1 teaspoon table salt
- ⅓ cup whole wheat flour
- 1 ½ to 1 ⅔ cups bread flour
- TOPPINGS
- 2 tablespoons olive oil
- 1 teaspoon Italian seasoning
- 1 clove garlic, minced
- ½ cup whole milk ricotta cheese, at room temperature
- ⅔ cup drained, chopped marinated artichokes
- ¼ cup chopped red onion
- 3 tablespoons minced fresh basil
- ½ cup shredded Parmesan cheese
- ⅓ cup shredded mozzarella cheese

Directions:
1. Make the Crust: Place the warm water, yeast, and sugar in a large mixing bowl for a stand mixer. Stir, then let stand for 3 to 5 minutes or until bubbly.
2. Stir in the olive oil, salt, whole wheat flour, and 1 ½ cups bread flour. If the dough is too sticky, stir in an additional 1 to 2 tablespoons bread flour. Beat with the flat (paddle) beater at medium-speed for 5 minutes (or knead by hand for 5 to 7 minutes or until the dough is smooth and elastic). Place in a greased large bowl, turn the dough over, cover with a clean towel, and let stand for 30 to 45 minutes, or until starting to rise.
3. Stir the olive oil, Italian seasoning, and garlic in a small bowl; set aside.
4. Preheat the toaster oven to 450°F. Place a 12-inch pizza pan in the toaster oven while it is preheating.
5. Turn the dough onto a lightly floured surface and pull or roll the dough to make a 12-inch circle. Carefully transfer the crust to the hot pan.
6. Brush the olive oil mixture over the crust. Spread the ricotta evenly over the crust. Top with the artichokes, red onions, fresh basil, Parmesan, and mozzarella. Bake for 13 to 15 minutes, or until the crust is golden brown and the cheese is melted. Let stand for 5 minutes before cutting.

Tarragon Beef Ragout

Servings: 6
Cooking Time: 53 Minutes
Ingredients:
- 1 pound lean round steak, cut across the grain of the meat into thin strips, approximately ¼ × 2 inches
- ½ cup dry red wine
- 1 small onion, chopped
- 2 carrots, peeled and thinly sliced
- 3 2 plum tomatoes, chopped
- 1 celery stalk, chopped
- 1 10-ounce package frozen peas
- 3 garlic gloves, minced
- 1 tablespoon Dijon mustard
- ½ teaspoon ground cumin
- ½ teaspoon dried tarragon
- Salt and freshly ground black pepper to taste

Directions:
1. Preheat the toaster oven to 375° F.
2. Combine all the ingredients with ½ cup water in an 8½ × 8½ × 4-inch ovenproof baking dish. Adjust the seasonings. Cover with aluminum foil.
3. BAKE, covered, for 45 minutes, or until the beef, onion, and celery are tender. Remove the cover.
4. BROIL 8 minutes to reduce the liquid and lightly brown the top.

Glazed Pork Tenderloin With Carrots Sheet Pan Supper

Servings: 4-6
Cooking Time: 20 Minutes
Ingredients:
- 1 pound pork tenderloin
- 1 teaspoon steak seasoning blend
- 2 large carrots, sliced 1/2-inch thick
- 2 large parsnips, sliced 1/2-inch thick
- 1/2 small sweet onion, cut in thin wedges
- 1 tablespoon olive oil
- Salt and pepper to taste
- 1/2 cup apricot jam
- 1 tablespoon balsamic vinegar

Directions:
1. Place rack on bottom position of toaster oven. Heat the toaster oven to 425°F. Spray the toaster oven baking pan with nonstick cooking spray or line the pan with nonstick aluminum foil.
2. Place pork tenderloin diagonally in center of pan. Sprinkle pork with seasoning blend.
3. In a large bowl, combine carrots, parsnips and onion. Add olive oil, salt and black pepper and stir until vegetables are coated. Arrange vegetables evenly in pan around pork.
4. Bake 20 minutes. Stir vegetables.
5. Meanwhile, in a small bowl, combine apricot jam and balsamic vinegar. Spoon about half of mixture over pork.
6. Continue baking until pork reaches reaches 160°F when tested with a meat thermometer and vegetables are roasted, about 10 minutes. Slice pork and serve with remaining sauce, if desired.

Chicken Gumbo

Servings: 4
Cooking Time: 40 Minutes
Ingredients:
- 2 skinless, boneless chicken breast halves, cut into 1-inch cubes
- ½ cup dry red wine
- 1 small onion, finely chopped
- 1 celery stalk, finely chopped
- 2 plum tomatoes, chopped
- 3 1 bell pepper, chopped
- 1 tablespoon minced fresh garlic
- 2 okra pods, stemmed, seeded, and finely chopped 1 bay leaf
- ½ teaspoon hot sauce
- ½ teaspoon dried thyme
- Salt and freshly ground black pepper to taste

Directions:
1. Preheat the toaster oven to 400° F.
2. Combine all the ingredients in a 1-quart 8½ × 8½ ×

4-inch ovenproof baking dish. Adjust the seasonings to taste. Cover with aluminum foil.
3. BAKE, covered, for 40 minutes, or until the onion, pepper, and celery are tender. Discard the bay leaf before serving.

One-step Classic Goulash

Servings: 4
Cooking Time: 56 Minutes
Ingredients:
- 1 cup elbow macaroni
- 1 cup (8-ounce can) tomato sauce
- 1 cup very lean ground round or sirloin
- 1 cup peeled and chopped fresh tomato
- ½ cup finely chopped onion
- 1 teaspoon garlic powder
- Salt and freshly ground black pepper
- Topping:
- 1 cup homemade bread crumbs
- 1 tablespoon margarine

Directions:
1. Preheat the toaster oven to 400° F.
2. Combine all the ingredients, except the topping, with 2 cups water in a 1-quart 8½ × 8½ × 4-inch ovenproof baking dish and mix well. Adjust the seasonings to taste. Cover with aluminum foil.
3. BAKE, covered, for 50 minutes, or until the macaroni is cooked, stirring after 25 minutes to distribute the liquid. Uncover, sprinkle with bread crumbs, and dot with margarine.
4. BROIL for 6 minutes, or until the topping is lightly browned.

Spanish Rice

Servings: 4
Cooking Time: 45 Minutes
Ingredients:
- ¾ cup rice
- 2 tablespoons dry white wine
- 3 tablespoons olive oil
- 1 15-ounce can whole tomatoes
- ¼ cup thinly sliced onions
- 3 tablespoons chopped fresh cilantro
- 4 ½ cup chopped bell pepper
- 5 2 bay leaves
- Salt and a pinch of red pepper flakes to taste

Directions:
1. Preheat the toaster oven to 375° F.
2. Combine all the ingredients with 1 cup water in a 1-quart 8½ × 8½ × 4-inch ovenproof baking dish and adjust the seasonings. Cover with aluminum foil.
3. BAKE, covered, for 45 minutes, or until the rice is cooked, removing the cover after 30 minutes.

Individual Baked Eggplant Parmesan

Servings: 5
Cooking Time: 55 Minutes

Ingredients:

- 1 medium eggplant, cut into 1/2-inch thick slices
- 1 1/2 teaspoons salt
- 1 cup Slow Cooker Marinara Sauce
- 1 package (8 oz.) fresh mozzarella, cut into 8 slices, divided
- 1 package (0.75 oz.) fresh basil, leaves only, divided
- 1/4 cup grated Parmesan cheese, divided

Directions:

1. Sprinkle eggplant with salt and place in a colander to drain for 1 hour.
2. Preheat the toaster oven to 375°F. Spray baking pan and 5 (4-inch) ramekins with nonstick cooking spray.
3. Rinse eggplant thoroughly with water to remove salt. Press each slice between paper towels to remove extra water and salt. Place on papertowels to dry. Arrange a single layer of eggplant slices in baking pan.
4. Bake 25 to 30 minutes or until eggplant is tender. Remove slices to cooking rack. Repeat baking remaining eggplant. Reduce oven temperature to 350°F.
5. In each ramekin, layer 1 slice eggplant, 1 tablespoon sauce, 1 slice mozzarella, 1 basil leaf, 1 additional tablespoon sauce and sprinkle with Parmesan cheese. Repeat layers ending with a sprinkle of Parmesan cheese.
6. Bake 20 to 25 minutes or until cheese is melted and eggplant layers are heated through.

Light Beef Stroganoff

Servings: 4
Cooking Time: 40 Minutes

Ingredients:

- Sauce:
- 1 cup skim milk
- 1 cup fat-free half-and-half
- 2 tablespoons reduced-fat cream cheese, at room temperature
- 4 tablespoons unbleached flour
- 2 pounds lean round or sirloin steak, cut into strips 2 inches long and ½ inch thick
- Browning mixture:
- 1 tablespoon soy sauce
- 2 tablespoons spicy brown mustard
- 1 tablespoon olive oil
- 2 teaspoons garlic powder
- Salt and freshly ground black pepper to taste

Directions:

1. Whisk together the sauce ingredients in a medium bowl until smooth. Set aside.
2. Combine the beef strips and browning mixture ingredients in an oiled or nonstick 8½ × 8½ × 2-inch square baking (cake) pan.
3. BROIL for 8 minutes, or until the strips are browned, turning with tongs after 4 minutes. Transfer to a 1-quart 8½ × 8½ × 4-inch ovenproof baking dish. Add the sauce and mix well. Adjust the seasonings to taste. Cover with aluminum foil.
4. BAKE, covered, for 40 minutes, or until the meat is tender.

French Bread Pizza

Servings: 6
Cooking Time: 8 Minutes

Ingredients:

- 2 tablespoons unsalted butter, melted
- 2 cloves garlic, minced
- ½ teaspoon Italian seasoning
- 1 tablespoon olive oil
- ½ cup chopped onion
- ½ cup chopped green pepper
- 1 cup sliced button or white mushrooms
- 1 (10- to 12-ounce) loaf French or Italian bread, about 12 inches long, split in half lengthwise
- ½ cup pizza sauce
- 6 to 8 slices Canadian bacon or ¼ cup pepperoni slices
- ¼ cup sliced ripe olives, drained
- 1 cup shredded mozzarella cheese
- 3 tablespoons shredded Parmesan cheese

Directions:

1. Preheat the toaster oven to 450°F.
2. Stir the melted butter, garlic, and Italian seasoning in a small bowl; set aside.
3. Heat the oil in a small skillet over medium-high heat. Add the onion and green pepper and sauté, stirring frequently, for 3 minutes. Add the mushrooms and cook, stirring frequently, for 7 to 10 minutes or until the liquid has evaporated. Remove from the heat; set aside.
4. Gently pull a little of the soft bread out of the center of the loaf, making a well. (Take care not to tear the crust.) Brush the garlic butter over the cut sides of the bread.
5. Place both halves of the bread, side by side, cut side up, on a 12 x 12-inch baking pan. Bake for 3 minutes or until heated through. Carefully remove the bread from the oven.
6. Spoon the pizza sauce evenly over the cut sides of the bread. Top evenly with the Canadian bacon, the onion-mushroom mixture, and the olives. Top with the mozzarella and Parmesan cheeses. Return to the oven and bake for 3 to 5 minutes or until the cheese is melted.
7. Cut the French bread pizza crosswise into slices.

Couscous-stuffed Poblano Peppers

Servings: 6
Cooking Time: 35 Minutes
Ingredients:
- 2 tablespoons olive oil
- ⅔ cup Israeli couscous
- 1 ¼ cups vegetable broth or water
- Kosher salt and freshly ground black pepper
- ½ medium onion, chopped
- 2 cloves garlic, minced
- 1 teaspoon dried oregano leaves
- ½ teaspoon ground cumin
- 1 (14.5-ounce) can fire-roasted diced tomatoes, with liquid
- Nonstick cooking spray
- 3 large poblano peppers, halved lengthwise, seeds and stem removed
- 1 ½ cups shredded Mexican blend, pepper Jack, or sharp cheddar cheese
- Optional toppings: minced fresh cilantro, sliced jalapeño peppers, diced tomatoes, sliced green onions (white and green portions)

Directions:
1. Heat 1 tablespoon oil in a medium saucepan over medium heat. Add the couscous and cook, stirring frequently, until golden brown, 2 to 3 minutes. Stir in the broth and season with salt and pepper. Cover, reduce the heat to a simmer, and cook, stirring occasionally, for about 10 minutes or until the liquid is absorbed. Remove from the heat and let stand, covered, for 5 minutes. Remove the cover, stir, and set aside to cool.
2. Heat the remaining 1 tablespoon oil in a small saucepan over medium heat. Add the onion, and cook, stirring frequently, for 3 to 5 minutes or until tender. Stir in the garlic and cook for 30 seconds. Stir in the oregano and cumin and season with salt and pepper. Stir in the tomatoes and simmer for 5 minutes.
3. Preheat the toaster oven to 400°F. Spray a 9-inch square baking pan with nonstick cooking spray. Spoon about one-third of the tomato mixture into the prepared pan. Arrange the peppers, cut side up, in the pan.
4. Stir 1 cup of the cheese into the couscous. Spoon the couscous mixture into the peppers, mounding slightly. Spoon the remaining tomato mixture over the peppers. Cover the pan and bake for 30 minutes.
5. Uncover the pan and sprinkle with the remaining cheese. Bake for 5 minutes or until the cheese is melted.
6. Top as desired with any of the various topping choices.

Sage, Chicken + Mushroom Pasta Casserole

Servings: 6
Cooking Time: 35 Minutes
Ingredients:
- Nonstick cooking spray
- 8 ounces bow-tie pasta, uncooked
- 4 tablespoons unsalted butter
- 8 ounces button or white mushrooms, sliced
- 3 tablespoons all-purpose flour
- Kosher salt and freshly ground black pepper
- 2 cups whole milk
- ½ cup dry white wine
- 2 tablespoons minced fresh sage
- 1 ½ cups chopped cooked chicken
- 1 cup shredded fontina, Monterey Jack, or Swiss cheese
- ½ cup shredded Parmesan cheese

Directions:
1. Preheat the toaster oven to 350°F. Spray a 2-quart baking pan with nonstick cooking spray.
2. Cook the pasta according to the package directions; drain and set aside.
3. Melt the butter in a large skillet over medium-high heat. Add the mushrooms and cook, stirring frequently, until the liquid has evaporated, 7 to 10 minutes. Blend in the flour and cook, stirring constantly, for 1 minute. Season with salt and pepper. Gradually stir in the milk and wine. Cook, stirring constantly, until the mixture bubbles and begins to thicken. Remove from the heat. Stir in the sage, cooked pasta, chicken, and fontina. Season with salt and pepper.
4. Spoon into the prepared pan. Cover and bake for 25 to 30 minutes. Uncover, sprinkle with the Parmesan, and bake for an additional 5 minutes or until the cheese is melted.
5. Remove from the oven and let stand for 5 to 10 minutes before serving.

Classic Tuna Casserole

Servings: 4
Cooking Time: 65 Minutes
Ingredients:
• 1 cup elbow macaroni
• 2 6-ounce cans tuna packed in water, drained well and crumbled
• 1 cup frozen peas 1 6-ounce can button mushrooms, drained
• 1 tablespoon margarine
• Salt and freshly ground black pepper
• 1 cup fat-free half-and-half
• 4 tablespoons unbleached flour
• 1 teaspoon garlic powder
• 1 cup multigrain bread crumbs
Directions:
1. Preheat the toaster oven to 400° F.
2. Combine the macaroni and 3 cups water in a 1-quart 8½ × 8½ × 4-inch ovenproof baking dish, stirring to blend well. Cover with aluminum foil.
3. BAKE, covered, for 35 minutes, or until the macaroni is tender. Remove from the oven and drain well. Return to the baking dish and add the tuna, peas, and mushrooms. Add salt and pepper to taste.
4. Whisk together the half-and-half, flour, and garlic powder in a small bowl until smooth. Add to the macaroni mixture and stir to blend well.
5. BAKE, covered, for 25 minutes. Remove from the oven, sprinkle the top with the bread crumbs, and dot with the margarine. Bake, uncovered, for 10 minutes, or until the top is browned.

Italian Bread Pizza

Servings: 4
Cooking Time: 30 Minutes
Ingredients:
• 1 loaf Italian or French bread, unsliced
• Filling:
• ½ cup tomato sauce
• 2 tablespoons tomato paste
• 2 tablespoons olive oil
• ½ cup grated zucchini
• ½ cup grated onion
• 2 tablespoons grated bell pepper
• 1 teaspoon garlic powder
• 2 tablespoons chopped pitted black olives
• 1 teaspoon dried oregano or 1 tablespoon chopped fresh oregano
• Salt to taste
• ¼ cup mozzarella cheese
Directions:
1. Preheat the toaster oven to 375° F.
2. Cut the loaf of bread in half lengthwise, then in quarters crosswise. Remove some of the bread from the center to make a cavity for the pizza topping.
3. Combine all the topping ingredients and spoon equal portions into the cavities in the bread. Sprinkle with mozzarella cheese. Place the bread quarters on the toaster oven rack.
4. BAKE for 30 minutes, or until the cheese is melted and the crust is lightly browned.

Middle Eastern Roasted Chicken

Servings: 4
Cooking Time: 25 Minutes
Ingredients:
• 3 tablespoons fresh lemon juice
• ¼ cup plus 1 tablespoon olive oil
• 4 cloves garlic, minced
• ½ teaspoon kosher salt
• 1 teaspoon freshly ground black pepper
• 1 teaspoon ground cumin
• 1 teaspoon paprika
• ½ teaspoon turmeric
• ⅛ teaspoon red pepper flakes
• 1 pound boneless, skinless chicken breasts
• 1 large onion, cut into thin wedges
Directions:
1. Whisk the lemon juice, ¼ cup olive oil, garlic, salt, pepper, cumin, paprika, turmeric, and red pepper flakes in a small bowl until blended.
2. Cut the chicken breast lengthwise into thin scaloppine slices. Place the chicken in a nonreactive dish and pour the marinade over the chicken. Turn the chicken to coat thoroughly and evenly. Cover, refrigerate, and marinate for at least 1 hour and up to 10 hours. (The longer the better, as the flavor melds with the chicken.)
3. Remove the chicken from the refrigerator and add the onion to the marinade.
4. Preheat the toaster oven to 425°F. Brush the remaining tablespoon of olive oil over the bottom of a 12 x 12-inch pan. Place the chicken pieces on one side of the baking sheet and the onion wedges on the other side in a single layer. Discard any remaining marinade.
5. Roast for 20 to 25 minutes or until the chicken is browned and a meat thermometer registers 165°F. Remove from the oven and let rest a few minutes, then slice the chicken into thin strips. Toss with the onion and serve.

Oven-baked Couscous

Servings: 4
Cooking Time: 10 Minutes
Ingredients:
- 1 10-ounce package couscous
- 2 tablespoons olive oil
- 2 tablespoons canned chickpeas
- 2 tablespoons canned or frozen green peas
- 1 tablespoon chopped fresh parsley
- 3 scallions, chopped
- Salt and pepper to taste

Directions:
1. Preheat the toaster oven to 400° F.
2. Mix together all the ingredients with 2 cups water in a 1-quart 8½ × 8½ × 4-inch ovenproof baking dish. Adjust the seasonings to taste. Cover with aluminum foil.
3. BAKE, covered, for 10 minutes, or until the couscous and vegetables are tender. Adjust the seasonings to taste and fluff with a fork before serving.

Family Favorite Pizza

Servings: 6
Cooking Time: 22 Minutes
Ingredients:
- CRUST
- ½ cup warm water (about 110 °F)
- 1 teaspoon active dry yeast
- 1 ½ cups all-purpose flour, plus more for kneading
- 1 teaspoon kosher salt
- ½ teaspoon olive oil
- TOPPINGS
- Pizza sauce
- 2 cups shredded Italian blend cheese or mozzarella cheese
- ¼ cup grated Parmesan cheese
- Optional toppings: pepperoni slices, cooked crumbled or sliced sausage, vegetables, or other favorite pizza toppings

Directions:
1. Make the Crust: Pour the water into a medium bowl and sprinkle with the yeast. Let stand for 5 minutes until the yeast is foamy. Add the flour, salt, and olive oil. Mix until a dough forms. Turn the dough out on a floured surface and knead until a ball forms that springs back when you poke a finger into it, about 5 minutes. If the dough is too sticky, add a tablespoon of flour and knead into the dough. Cover the dough and allow to rest for 10 minutes.
2. Preheat the toaster oven to 450°F. Place a 12-inch pizza pan in the toaster oven while it is preheating.
3. Stretch and roll the dough into an 11 ½-inch round. If the dough starts to shrink back, let it rest for 5 to 10 more minutes and then continue to roll. Carefully remove the hot pan from the toaster oven and place the pizza crust on the hot pan. Top with the desired amount of sauce. Layer cheese and any of your favorite pizza toppings over the pizza.

4. Bake for 18 to 22 minutes, or until the crust is golden brown and the cheese is melted. Let stand for 5 minutes before cutting.

Slow Cooker Chicken Philly Cheesesteak Sandwich

Servings: 4
Cooking Time: 2 Minutes
Ingredients:
- 1 3/4 to 2 pounds chicken tenders
- 2 large green peppers, cut in strips
- 2 medium onions, sliced
- 1 1/2 tablespoons rotisserie seasoning
- 1/2 teaspoon salt
- 4 tablespoons Italian salad dressing
- 4 hoagie rolls, split
- 4 slices Cheddar or American cheese
- 1/4 cup banana pepper rings, optional
- Hot Sauce or ketchup, optional

Directions:
1. In slow cooker crock, combine chicken tenders, pepper strips and onion slices with rotisserie seasoning and salt.
2. Cook on HIGH for 2 to 2 1/2 hours or LOW for 4 to 5 hours.
3. Preheat the toaster oven broiler. Open rolls and place on a cookie sheet
4. Slice chicken tenders. Place back in slow cooker. With a slotted spoon, divide chicken, peppers and onions among rolls and drizzle with Italian dressing. Top with cheese slices.
5. Place under broiler until cheese is melted, about 2 minutes.
6. Serve with banana peppers, hot sauce or ketchup, if desired.

Lentil And Carrot Soup

Servings: 4
Cooking Time: 40 Minutes
Ingredients:
- ½ cup lentils
- ½ cup dry white wine
- 1 small onion, chopped
- 3 carrots, peeled and finely chopped
- ½ cup fresh mushrooms, cleaned and sliced, or 1 5-ounce can mushroom pieces, well drained
- 3 garlic cloves, minced
- 1 tablespoon chopped fresh parsley
- 1 tablespoon Worcestershire sauce
- Salt and freshly ground black pepper to taste

Directions:
1. Preheat the toaster oven to 375° F.
2. Combine all the ingredients with 2 cups water in a 1-quart 8½ × 8½ × 4-inch ovenproof baking dish. Adjust

the seasonings.

3. BAKE for 40 minutes, or until the lentils, carrots, and onions are tender. Ladle into individual soup bowls and serve.

Dijon Salmon With Green Beans Sheet Pan Supper

Servings: 2-3
Cooking Time: 15 Minutes
Ingredients:
- 3/4 pound salmon fillets, cut in portion-size pieces
- 2 tablespoons olive oil
- 1 tablespoon soy sauce
- 1 tablespoon Dijon mustard
- 2 cloves garlic
- 6 ounces thin green beans, trimmed
- 1/2 small red bell pepper, thinly sliced
- 1/2 small yellow bell pepper, thinly sliced
- 1 small leek, white part only, thinly sliced
- Dash coarse black pepper

Directions:
1. Place rack on bottom position of toaster oven. Preheat the toaster oven to 400°F. Spray the toaster oven baking pan with nonstick cooking spray or line the pan with nonstick aluminum foil. Place salmon skin-side down in center of pan.
2. In a food chopper, process olive oil, soy sauce, mustard and garlic until blended and garlic is chopped. Set aside.
3. In a large bowl, combine green beans, bell peppers and leeks. Add 2 tablespoons olive oil mixture and stir until vegetables are coated. Arrange vegetables evenly in pan around salmon.
4. Drizzle salmon with remaining olive oil mixture.
5. Bake until salmon is done to medium-well and vegetables are crisp-tender, about 15 minutes.

Broiled Chipotle Tilapia With Avocado Sauce

Servings: 2
Cooking Time: 10 Minutes
Ingredients:
- 1 small avocado, halved, pitted and peeled
- 3 tablespoons sour cream
- 1 teaspoon lime juice
- 2 1/2 teaspoons chipotle and roasted garlic seasoning, divided
- 1 tablespoon mayonnaise
- 1/2 pound tilapia fillets
- Chopped cilantro

Directions:
1. Using a chopper or small food processor, blend avocado, sour cream, lime juice and 1 1/2 teaspoons seasoning until

smooth. Cover and refrigerate.
2. Spray toaster oven baking pan with nonstick cooking spray.
3. in small bowl, mix mayonnaise and remaining 1 teaspoon seasoning.
4. Brush mayonnaise mixture on both sides of tilapia fillets.
5. Place coated fish in pan.
6. Set toaster oven to BROIL. Broil fish for 10 minutes or until fish flakes with a fork.
7. Serve with avocado sauce and garnish with lime slices and cilantro, if desired.

Easy Oven Lasagne

Servings: 4
Cooking Time: 60 Minutes
Ingredients:
- 6 uncooked lasagna noodles, broken in half
- 1 15-ounce jar marinara sauce
- ½ pound ground turkey or chicken breast
- ½ cup part-skim ricotta cheese
- ½ cup shredded part-skim mozzarella cheese
- 2 tablespoons chopped fresh oregano leaves or 1 teaspoon dried oregano
- 2 tablespoons chopped fresh basil leaves or 1 teaspoon dried basil
- 1 tablespoon garlic cloves, minced
- ¼ cup grated Parmesan cheese
- Salt and freshly ground black pepper to taste

Directions:
1. Preheat the toaster oven to 375° F.
2. Layer in a 1-quart 8½ × 8½ × 4-inch ovenproof baking dish in this order: 6 lasagna noodle halves, ½ jar of the marinara sauce, ½ cup water, half of the ground meat, half of the ricotta and mozzarella cheeses, half of the oregano and basil leaves, and half of the minced garlic. Repeat the layer, starting with the noodles. Cover the dish with aluminum foil.
3. BAKE, covered, for 50 minutes, or until the noodles are tender. Uncover, sprinkle the top with Parmesan cheese and bake for another 10 minutes, or until the liquid is reduced and the top is browned.

Cornucopia Casserole

Servings: 4
Cooking Time: 45 Minutes
Ingredients:
- 1 celery stalk, chopped
- 2 tablespoons chopped Vidalia onion
- 3 ½ bell pepper, chopped
- 1 carrot, peeled and chopped
- 1 small zucchini, chopped
- ½ cup green beans, cut into 1-inch Pieces
- ½ cup frozen peas ½ cup frozen corn
- ½ cup frozen broccoli florets
- ½ cup frozen cauliflower florets
- 2 tablespoons vegetable oil
- 1 teaspoon ground cumin
- 1 teaspoon garlic powder
- ½ teaspoon paprika
- Salt and freshly ground black pepper to taste
- ½ cup finely chopped pecans
- 3 tablespoons grated Parmesan cheese

Directions:
1. Preheat the toaster oven to 400° F.
2. Combine all the ingredients, except the pecans and Parmesan cheese, in a 1-quart 8½ × 8½ × 4-inch ovenproof baking dish and adjust the seasonings to taste. Cover with aluminum foil.
3. BAKE, covered, for 35 minutes, or until the vegetables are tender. Uncover, stir to distribute the liquid, and adjust the seasonings again. Sprinkle the top with the pecans and Parmesan cheese.
4. BROIL for 10 minutes, or until the pecans are lightly browned.

Oven-baked Barley

Servings: 2
Cooking Time: 60 Minutes
Ingredients:
- ⅓ cup barley, toasted
- Seasonings:
- 1 tablespoon sesame oil
- 1 tablespoon sesame seeds
- ¼ teaspoon ground cumin
- ¼ teaspoon turmeric
- ½ teaspoon garlic powder
- Salt and freshly ground black pepper to taste

Directions:
1. Combine the barley and 1½ cups water in a 1-quart 8½ × 8½ × 4-inch ovenproof baking dish. Cover with aluminum foil.
2. BAKE, covered, for 50 minutes, or until almost cooked, testing the grains after 30 minutes for softness.
3. Add the oil and seasonings and fluff with a fork to combine. Cover and let the barley sit for 10 minutes to finish

cooking and absorb the flavors of the seasonings. Fluff once more before serving.

Homemade Pizza Sauce

Servings: 1
Cooking Time: 20 Minutes
Ingredients:
- 1 9-inch ready-made pizza crust or 1 homemade pizza crust
- 2 plum tomatoes, chopped
- 1 tablespoon olive oil
- 3 garlic cloves, peeled and chopped ¼ cup chopped onion
- 2 tablespoons tomato paste
- 2 tablespoons dry red wine
- 1 tablespoon chopped fresh basil or 1 teaspoon dried basil
- 1 tablespoon chopped fresh oregano or 1 teaspoon dried oregano
- 1 bay leaf
- Salt and freshly ground black pepper to taste

Directions:
1. Combine all ingredients in an 8½ × 8½ × 2-inch square baking (cake) pan. Adjust the seasonings to taste.
2. BROIL for 20 minutes, or until the onions and tomatoes are tender. Remove the bay leaf and cool before spreading on the pizza crust. Bake the pizza according to instructions on the ready-made crust package or in the homemade pizza crust recipe.

Tomato Bisque

Servings: 4
Cooking Time: 25 Minutes
Ingredients:
- 1 8-ounce can tomato sauce
- 1 7-ounce jar diced pimientos, drained
- 1 tablespoon finely chopped onion
- 2 cups low-fat buttermilk
- 1 cup fat-free half-and-half
- 1 tablespoon low-fat cream cheese
- 1 teaspoon garlic powder
- ½ teaspoon paprika
- ½ teaspoon ground bay leaf
- 1 teaspoon hot sauce (optional)
- Salt and white pepper to taste
- 2 tablespoons minced fresh basil leaves

Directions:
1. Preheat the toaster oven to 350° F.
2. Process all the ingredients except the basil in a blender or food processor until smooth. Pour into a 1-quart 8½ × 8½ × 4-inch ovenproof baking dish. Adjust the seasonings to taste.
3. BAKE, covered, for 25 minutes. Ladle into small soup bowls and garnish each with fresh basil leaves before serving.

Connecticut Garden Chowder

Servings: 4

Cooking Time: 60 Minutes

Ingredients:
- Soup:
- ½ cup peeled and shredded potato
- ½ cup shredded carrot
- ½ cup shredded celery 2 plum tomatoes, chopped
- 1 small zucchini, shredded
- 2 bay leaves
- ¼ teaspoon sage
- 1 teaspoon garlic powder
- Salt and butcher's pepper to taste
- Chowder base:
- 2 tablespoons reduced-fat cream cheese, at room temperature
- ½ cup fat-free half-and-half
- 2 tablespoons unbleached flour
- 2 tablespoons chopped fresh parsley

Directions:

1. Preheat the toaster oven to 375° F.

2. Combine the soup ingredients in a 1-quart 8½ × 8½ × 4-inch ovenproof baking dish, mixing well. Adjust the seasonings to taste.

3. BAKE, covered, for 40 minutes, or until the vegetables are tender.

4. Whisk the chowder mixture ingredients together until smooth. Add the mixture to the cooked soup ingredients and stir well to blend.

5. BAKE, uncovered for 20 minutes, or until the stock is thickened. Ladle the soup into individual soup bowls and garnish with the parsley.

Honey-glazed Ginger Pork Meatballs

Servings: 6

Cooking Time: 20 Minutes

Ingredients:
- 1 ½ pounds ground pork
- 2 tablespoons finely chopped onion
- 3 cloves garlic, minced
- 1 teaspoon minced fresh ginger
- 1 teaspoon sesame oil
- 1 large egg
- 3 tablespoons panko bread crumbs
- Kosher salt and freshly ground black pepper
- HONEY GINGER SAUCE
- 2 tablespoons sesame oil
- 1 tablespoon canola or vegetable oil
- 3 cloves garlic, minced
- 1 ½ tablespoons minced fresh ginger
- 3 tablespoons unseasoned rice wine vinegar
- 1 tablespoon reduced-sodium soy sauce
- 3 tablespoons honey
- 2 to 3 teaspoons garlic chili sauce
- 1 teaspoon cornstarch
- 1 tablespoon cold water
- 2 tablespoons minced fresh cilantro

Directions:

1. Preheat the toaster oven to 375°F. Line a 12 x 12-inch baking pan with nonstick aluminum foil (or if lining the pan with regular foil, spray it with nonstick cooking spray).

2. Combine the pork, onion, garlic, ginger, sesame oil, egg, and panko bread crumbs in a large bowl. Season with salt and pepper. Form into meatballs about 1 ½ inches in diameter. Place the meatballs in the prepared baking pan. Bake for 18 to 20 minutes or until done and a meat thermometer registers 160°F.

3. Make the Honey Ginger Sauce: Combine the sesame oil, canola oil, garlic, and ginger in a medium skillet over medium-high heat. Cook, stirring frequently, for 1 minute. Add the vinegar, soy sauce, honey, and chili sauce and bring to a boil. Whisk the cornstarch with the water in a small bowl. Stir the cornstarch mixture into the sauce and cook, stirring constantly, until thickened. Add the meatballs to the skillet and coat with the sauce. Sprinkle with the cilantro for serving.

Desserts

Desserts

Donut Holes

Servings: 13
Cooking Time: 12 Minutes

Ingredients:
- 6 tablespoons Granulated white sugar
- 1½ tablespoons Butter, melted and cooled
- 2 tablespoons (or 1 small egg, well beaten) Pasteurized egg substitute, such as Egg Beaters
- 6 tablespoons Regular or low-fat sour cream (not fat-free)
- ¾ teaspoon Vanilla extract
- 1⅔ cups All-purpose flour
- ¾ teaspoon Baking powder
- ¼ teaspoon Table salt
- Vegetable oil spray

Directions:
1. Preheat the toaster oven to 350°F .
2. Whisk the sugar and melted butter in a medium bowl until well combined. Whisk in the egg substitute or egg , then the sour cream and vanilla until smooth. Remove the whisk and stir in the flour, baking powder, and salt with a wooden spoon just until a soft dough forms.
3. Use 2 tablespoons of this dough to create a ball between your clean palms. Set it aside and continue making balls: 8 more for the small batch, 12 more for the medium batch, or 17 more for the large one.
4. Coat the balls in the vegetable oil spray, then set them in the air fryer oven with as much air space between them as possible. Even a fraction of an inch will be enough, but they should not touch. Air-fry undisturbed for 12 minutes, or until browned and cooked through. A toothpick inserted into the center of a ball should come out clean.
5. Pour the contents of the air fryer oven onto a wire rack. Cool for at least 5 minutes before serving.

Heritage Chocolate Chip Cookies

Servings: 16-18
Cooking Time: 12 Minutes

Ingredients:
- 1 1/2 cups all-purpose flour
- 1 teaspoon baking powder
- 1/2 teaspoon salt
- 1 large egg, unbeaten
- 1/2 cup shortening
- 1/2 cup packed dark brown sugar
- 1/4 cup granulated sugar
- 2 teaspoons vanilla extract
- 1 tablespoon milk
- 1 cup chocolate chips

Directions:
1. Preheat the toaster oven to 375°F.
2. Place all ingredients except chocolate chips in large mixer bowl. With electric mixer on low speed, beat until ingredients are mixed. Gradually increase speed to medium and beat 3 minutes, stopping to scrape bowl as needed.
3. Add chocolate chips and beat on low until blended.
4. Line cookie sheets with parchment paper. Using a small scoop, place 12 scoops of cookie dough about 1-inch apart on parchment.
5. Bake 10 to 12 minutes or until cookies are browned. Slide parchment with baked cookies onto rack to cool. Repeat with remaining dough.

Black And Blue Clafoutis

Servings: 2
Cooking Time: 15 Minutes

Ingredients:
- 6-inch pie pan
- 3 large eggs
- ½ cup sugar
- 1 teaspoon vanilla extract
- 2 tablespoons butter, melted 1 cup milk
- ½ cup all-purpose flour
- 1 cup blackberries
- 1 cup blueberries
- 2 tablespoons confectioners' sugar

Directions:
1. Preheat the toaster oven to 320°F.
2. Combine the eggs and sugar in a bowl and whisk vigorously until smooth, lighter in color and well combined. Add the vanilla extract, butter and milk and whisk together well. Add the flour and whisk just until no lumps or streaks of white remain.
3. Scatter half the blueberries and blackberries in a greased (6-inch) pie pan or cake pan. Pour half of the batter (about 1¼ cups) on top of the berries and transfer the tart pan to the air fryer oven. You can use an aluminum foil sling to help with this by taking a long piece of aluminum foil, folding it in half lengthwise twice until it is roughly 26-inches by 3-inches. Place this under the pie dish and hold the ends of the foil to move the pie dish in and out of the air fryer oven. Tuck the ends of the foil beside the pie dish while it cooks in the air fryer oven.
4. Air-fry at 320°F for 15 minutes or until the clafoutis has puffed up and is still a little jiggly in the center. Remove the clafoutis from the air fryer oven, invert it onto a plate and let it cool while you bake the second batch. Serve the cla-

foutis warm, dusted with confectioners' sugar on top.

Key Lime Pie

Servings: 8
Cooking Time: 60 Minutes
Ingredients:
- FILLING
- 1 (14-ounce) can sweetened condensed milk
- 4 large egg yolks
- 4 teaspoons grated lime zest plus ½ cup juice (5 limes)
- CRUST
- 11 whole graham crackers, broken into 1-inch pieces
- 3 tablespoons granulated sugar
- 5 tablespoons unsalted butter, melted and cooled
- TOPPING
- ¾ cup heavy cream
- ¼ cup (1 ounce) confectioners' sugar

Directions:
1. FOR THE FILLING: Whisk condensed milk, egg yolks, and lime zest and juice together in bowl until smooth. Cover mixture and let sit at room temperature until thickened, about 30 minutes.
2. FOR THE CRUST: Adjust toaster oven rack to middle position and preheat the toaster oven to 325 degrees. Process graham cracker pieces and sugar in food processor to fine, even crumbs, about 30 seconds. Sprinkle melted butter over crumbs and pulse to incorporate, about 5 pulses.
3. Sprinkle mixture into 9-inch pie plate. Using bottom of dry measuring cup, press crumbs into even layer on bottom and up sides of pie plate. Bake until crust is fragrant and beginning to brown, 10 to 15 minutes. Transfer to wire rack and let cool slightly, about 10 minutes.
4. Pour thickened filling into warm crust and smooth top. Bake pie until center is firm but jiggles slightly when shaken, 12 to 17 minutes. Let pie cool slightly on wire rack, about 1 hour. Cover pie loosely with plastic wrap and refrigerate until filling is chilled and set, at least 3 hours or up to 24 hours.
5. For the topping Using stand mixer fitted with whisk attachment, whip cream and sugar on medium-low speed until foamy, about 1 minute. Increase speed to high and whip until soft peaks form, 1 to 3 minutes. (Topping can be refrigerated in fine-mesh strainer set over small bowl and covered with plastic wrap for up to 8 hours.) Spread whipped cream attractively over pie. Serve.

Midnight Nutella® Banana Sandwich

Servings: 2
Cooking Time: 8 Minutes
Ingredients:
- butter, softened
- 4 slices white bread
- ¼ cup chocolate hazelnut spread (Nutella®)
- 1 banana

Directions:
1. Preheat the toaster oven to 370°F.
2. Spread the softened butter on one side of all the slices of bread and place the slices buttered side down on the counter. Spread the chocolate hazelnut spread on the other side of the bread slices. Cut the banana in half and then slice each half into three slices lengthwise. Place the banana slices on two slices of bread and top with the remaining slices of bread (buttered side up) to make two sandwiches. Cut the sandwiches in half (triangles or rectangles) – this will help them all fit in the air fryer oven at once. Transfer the sandwiches to the air fryer oven.
3. Air-fry at 370°F for 5 minutes. Flip the sandwiches over and air-fry for another 2 to 3 minutes, or until the top bread slices are nicely browned. Pour yourself a glass of milk or a midnight nightcap while the sandwiches cool slightly and enjoy!

Apricot Coffee Cake

Servings: 1
Cooking Time: 15 Minutes
Ingredients:
- 2 cups baking mix
- 3 ounces cream cheese
- ¼ cup unsalted butter
- ½ cup chopped pecans, toasted
- ⅓ cup whole milk
- ¾ cup apricot preserves
- GLAZE
- 1 cup confectioners' sugar
- ¼ teaspoon almond extract
- 1 to 2 tablespoons whole milk

Directions:
1. Preheat the toaster oven to 425 °F. Grease a 12 x 12-inch baking pan.
2. Place the baking mix in a large bowl. Using a pastry cutter or two knives, cut the cream cheese and butter into the baking mix until the mixture is crumbly throughout. Add the pecans and milk and mix well.
3. Turn the dough onto a lightly floured surface and knead lightly about 8 times. Roll the dough into a 12 x 8-inch rectangle. Place the rolled dough diagonally on the prepared pan. Spread the preserves lengthwise down the center of the dough. Make 2 ½-inch cuts at 1-inch intervals on both sides of the filling. Fold the strips over the preserves, overlapping in the center. Bake for 15 minutes or until golden brown.
4. Make the Glaze: Whisk the confectioners' sugar, almond extract, and 1 tablespoon milk in a small bowl until smooth. Add additional milk, as needed, to make a glaze consistency.
5. Drizzle the glaze over the warm coffee cake.

Gingerbread

Servings: 6
Cooking Time: 20 Minutes
Ingredients:
- cooking spray
- 1 cup flour
- 2 tablespoons sugar
- ¾ teaspoon ground ginger
- ¼ teaspoon cinnamon
- 1 teaspoon baking powder
- ½ teaspoon baking soda
- ⅛ teaspoon salt
- 1 egg
- ¼ cup molasses
- ½ cup buttermilk
- 2 tablespoons oil
- 1 teaspoon pure vanilla extract

Directions:
1. Preheat the toaster oven to 330°F.
2. Spray 6 x 6-inch baking dish lightly with cooking spray.
3. In a medium bowl, mix together all the dry ingredients.
4. In a separate bowl, beat the egg. Add molasses, buttermilk, oil, and vanilla and stir until well mixed.
5. Pour liquid mixture into dry ingredients and stir until well blended.
6. Pour batter into baking dish and Air-fry at 330°F for 20 minutes or until toothpick inserted in center of loaf comes out clean.

Lime Cheesecake

Servings: 6
Cooking Time: 30 Minutes
Ingredients:
- Oil spray (hand-pumped)
- ½ cup graham cracker crumbs
- 24 ounces cream cheese, room temperature
- 1½ cups granulated sugar
- 4 large eggs
- ¼ cup sour cream
- Juice and zest of 1 lime
- 2 teaspoons vanilla extract

Directions:
1. Place the rack in position 1 and preheat the oven to 350°F on BAKE for 5 minutes.
2. Lightly spray an 8-inch springform pan with the oil and spread the graham cracker crumbs in the bottom.
3. Bake for 10 minutes, then remove the crust from the air fryer and set it aside.
4. In a large bowl, beat the cream cheese until very smooth with an electric hand beater. Add the sugar by ½-cup measures, beating very well after each addition and scraping down the sides of the bowl.
5. Add the eggs one at a time, beating well after each addi-

tion and scraping down the sides of the bowl.
6. Beat in the sour cream, lime juice, lime zest, and vanilla until very well blended and fluffy, about 4 minutes.
7. Transfer the batter to the pan and smooth the top.
8. Bake for 30 minutes or until set.
9. Let the cheesecake cool in the oven for 30 minutes and then transfer to the refrigerator to cool completely. Serve.

Cheese Blintzes

Servings: 6
Cooking Time: 10 Minutes
Ingredients:
- 1½ 7½-ounce package(s) farmer cheese
- 3 tablespoons Regular or low-fat cream cheese (not fat-free)
- 3 tablespoons Granulated white sugar
- ¼ teaspoon Vanilla extract
- 6 Egg roll wrappers
- 3 tablespoons Butter, melted and cooled

Directions:
1. Preheat the toaster oven to 375°F.
2. Use a flatware fork to mash the farmer cheese, cream cheese, sugar, and vanilla in a small bowl until smooth.
3. Set one egg roll wrapper on a clean, dry work surface. Place ¼ cup of the filling at the edge closest to you, leaving a ½-inch gap before the edge of the wrapper. Dip your clean finger in water and wet the edges of the wrapper. Fold the perpendicular sides over the filling, then roll the wrapper closed with the filling inside. Set it aside seam side down and continue filling the remainder of the wrappers.
4. Brush the wrappers on all sides with the melted butter. Be generous. Set them seam side down in the air fryer oven with as much space between them as possible. Air-fry undisturbed for 10 minutes, or until lightly browned.
5. Use a nonstick-safe spatula to transfer the blintzes to a wire rack. Cool for at least 5 minutes or up to 20 minutes before serving.

Almond-roasted Pears

Servings: 4
Cooking Time: 15 Minutes
Ingredients:
- Yogurt Topping
- 1 container vanilla Greek yogurt (5–6 ounces)
- ¼ teaspoon almond flavoring
- 2 whole pears
- ¼ cup crushed Biscoff cookies (approx. 4 cookies)
- 1 tablespoon sliced almonds
- 1 tablespoon butter

Directions:
1. Stir almond flavoring into yogurt and set aside while preparing pears.
2. Halve each pear and spoon out the core.

3. Place pear halves in air fryer oven.

4. Stir together the cookie crumbs and almonds. Place a quarter of this mixture into the hollow of each pear half.

5. Cut butter into 4 pieces and place one piece on top of crumb mixture in each pear.

6. Preheat the toaster oven to 400°F and air-fry for 15 minutes or until pears have cooked through but are still slightly firm.

7. Serve pears warm with a dollop of yogurt topping.

Baked Custard

Servings: 2
Cooking Time: 45 Minutes
Ingredients:
- 2 eggs
- ¼ cup sugar
- 1 cup low-fat evaporated milk
- ½ teaspoon vanilla extract
- Pinch of grated nutmeg
- Fat-free half-and-half

Directions:

1. Preheat the toaster oven to 350° F.

2. Beat together the eggs, sugar, milk, vanilla, and nutmeg in a small bowl with an electric mixer at medium speed. Pour equal portions of the custard mixture into 2 oiled 1-cup-size ovenproof dishes.

3. BAKE for 45 minutes, or until a toothpick inserted in the center comes out clean. Serve drizzled with warm fat-free half-and-half.

Campfire Banana Boats

Servings: 4
Cooking Time: 20 Minutes
Ingredients:
- 4 medium, unpeeled ripe bananas
- ¼ cup dark chocolate chips
- 4 teaspoons shredded, unsweetened coconut
- ½ cup mini marshmallows
- 4 graham crackers, chopped

Directions:

1. Preheat the toaster oven to 400°F on BAKE for 5 minutes.

2. Cut the bananas lengthwise through the skin about halfway through. Open the pocket to create a space for the other ingredients.

3. Evenly divide the chocolate, coconut, marshmallows, and graham crackers among the bananas.

4. Tear off four 12-inch squares of foil and place the bananas in the center of each. Crimp the foil around the banana to form a boat.

5. Place the bananas on the baking tray, two at a time, and in position 2, bake for 10 minutes until the fillings are gooey and the banana is warmed through.

6. Repeat with the remaining two bananas and serve.

Lemon Torte

Servings: 6
Cooking Time: 16 Minutes
Ingredients:
- First mixture:
- ¼ cup margarine, at room temperature
- ½ teaspoon grated lemon zest
- 3 egg yolks
- ¼ cup sugar
- ⅓ cup unbleached flour
- 3 tablespoons cornstarch
- Second mixture:
- 3 egg whites
- 2 tablespoons sugar
- Cream Cheese Frosting (recipe follows)

Directions:

1. Beat together the first mixture ingredients in a medium bowl with an electric mixer until the mixture is smooth. Set aside. Clean the electric mixer beaters.

2. Beat the second mixture together: Beat the egg whites into soft peaks in a medium bowl, gradually adding the sugar, and continue beating until the peaks are stiff. Fold the first mixture into the second mixture to make the torte batter.

3. Pour ½ cup torte batter into a small oiled or nonstick 3½ × 7½ × 2¼-inch loaf pan.

4. BROIL for 1 or 2 minutes, or until lightly browned. Remove from the oven.

5. Pour and spread evenly another ½ cup batter on top of the first layer. Broil again for 1 or 2 minutes, or until lightly browned. Repeat the process until all the batter is used up. When cool, run a knife around the sides to loosen and invert onto a plate. Chill. Frost with Cream Cheese Frosting and serve chilled.

Apple Juice Piecrust

Servings: 4
Cooking Time: 10 Minutes
Ingredients:
- 1¼ cups unbleached flour
- ¼ cup margarine
- ¼ cup apple juice
- Pinch of grated nutmeg
- Salt to taste

Directions:

1. Preheat the toaster oven to 350° F.

2. Cut together the flour and margarine with a knife or pastry cutter until the mixture is crumbly. Add the apple juice, nutmeg, and salt and cut again to blend. Turn the dough out onto a lightly floured surface and knead for 2 minutes. Roll out into a circle large enough to fit a 9¾-inch pie pan.

Pierce in several places to prevent bubbling and press the tines of a fork around the rim to decorate the crust edge.

3. BAKE for 10 minutes, or until lightly browned.

Meringue Topping

Servings: 1
Cooking Time: 12 Minutes
Ingredients:
- 3 egg whites
- 1 cup sugar

Directions:
1. Beat the egg whites and sugar together in a medium bowl until the mixture is stiff. Spread on top of the pie.
2. BAKE at 375°F. for 12 minutes, or until the meringue topping is browned.

Cranapple Crisp

Servings: 6
Cooking Time: 35 Minutes
Ingredients:
- 2 apples, peeled, cored, and diced
- 3 cups chopped fresh or thawed frozen cranberries
- ¼ cup brown sugar
- ¼ cup wheat germ
- 1 tablespoon margarine
- 1 tablespoon vegetable oil
- ½ cup brown sugar
- 1 teaspoon ground cinnamon
- ¼ teaspoon grated nutmeg
- Salt to taste

Directions:
1. Preheat the toaster oven to 350° F.
2. Combine the cranberries, apples, and sugar in a large bowl, mixing well. Transfer to an oiled or nonstick 8½ × 8½ × 2-inch square baking (cake) pan. Set aside.
3. Combine the topping ingredients in a medium bowl, stirring with a fork until crumbly. Sprinkle evenly on top of the cranberry/apple mixture.
4. BAKE for 35 minutes, or until the top is golden brown.

Almost Sinless Pear Banana Bread Pudding

Servings: 4
Cooking Time: 40 Minutes
Ingredients:
- 1 cup peeled and sliced fresh pears or 1 cup sliced canned pears, well drained
- 1 banana
- 1 cup skim milk
- 1 egg
- 2 tablespoons light brown sugar
- ¼ teaspoon salt ½ teaspoon ground cinnamon

- 2 cups toast, cut into 1 × 1-inch cubes or pieces

Directions:
1. Preheat the toaster oven to 400° F.
2. Blend the pears, banana, milk, egg, sugar, salt, and cinnamon in a food processor or blender until smooth. Transfer to an 8½ × 8½ × 4-inch ovenproof baking dish. Add the toast and mix well.
3. BAKE for 40 minutes, or until the center is firm and lightly browned. Cool and top with whipped cream, ice cream, nuts, or fresh or canned berries.

Carrot Cake

Servings: 6
Cooking Time: 30 Minutes
Ingredients:
- FOR THE CAKE
- ½ cup canola oil, plus extra for greasing the baking dish
- 1 cup all-purpose flour, plus extra for dusting the baking dish
- 1 cup granulated sugar
- 1 teaspoon baking powder
- ½ teaspoon sea salt
- 2 teaspoons pumpkin pie spice
- 2 large eggs
- 1 cup carrot, finely shredded
- ½ cup dried apricot, chopped
- FOR THE ICING
- 4 ounces cream cheese, room temperature
- ¼ cup salted butter, room temperature
- 1 teaspoon vanilla extract
- 2 cups confectioners' sugar

Directions:
1. To make the cake
2. Place the rack in position 1 and preheat the oven to 325°F on BAKE for 5 minutes.
3. Lightly grease an 8-inch-square baking dish with oil and dust with flour.
4. Place the rack in position 1.
5. In a large bowl, stir the flour, sugar, baking powder, salt, and pumpkin pie spice.
6. Make a well in the center and add the oil and eggs, stirring until just combined. Add the carrot and apricot and stir until well mixed.
7. Transfer the batter to the baking dish and bake for about 30 minutes until golden brown and a toothpick inserted in the center comes out clean.
8. Remove the cake from the oven and cool completely in the baking dish.
9. To make the icing
10. When the cake is cool, whisk the cream cheese, butter, and vanilla until very smooth and blended. Add the confectioners' sugar and whisk until creamy and thick, about 2 minutes.
11. Ice the cake and serve.

Giant Buttery Oatmeal Cookie

Servings: 4
Cooking Time: 16 Minutes
Ingredients:
- 1 cup Rolled oats (not quick-cooking or steel-cut oats)
- ½ cup All-purpose flour
- ½ teaspoon Baking soda
- ½ teaspoon Ground cinnamon
- ½ teaspoon Table salt
- 3½ tablespoons Butter, at room temperature
- ⅓ cup Packed dark brown sugar
- 1½ tablespoons Granulated white sugar
- 3 tablespoons (or 1 medium egg, well beaten) Pasteurized egg substitute, such as Egg Beaters
- ¾ teaspoon Vanilla extract
- ⅓ cup Chopped pecans
- Baking spray

Directions:
1. Preheat the toaster oven to 350°F.
2. Stir the oats, flour, baking soda, cinnamon, and salt in a bowl until well combined.
3. Using an electric hand mixer at medium speed , beat the butter, brown sugar, and granulated white sugar until creamy and thick, about 3 minutes, scraping down the inside of the bowl occasionally. Beat in the egg substitute or egg (as applicable) and vanilla until uniform.
4. Scrape down and remove the beaters. Fold in the flour mixture and pecans with a rubber spatula just until all the flour is moistened and the nuts are even throughout the dough.
5. For a small air fryer oven, coat the inside of a 6-inch round cake pan with baking spray. For a medium air fryer oven, coat the inside of a 7-inch round cake pan with baking spray. And for a large air fryer oven, coat the inside of an 8-inch round cake pan with baking spray. Scrape and gently press the dough into the prepared pan, spreading it into an even layer to the perimeter.
6. Set the pan in the toaster oven and air-fry undisturbed for 16 minutes, or until puffed and browned.
7. Transfer the pan to a wire rack and cool for 10 minutes. Loosen the cookie from the perimeter with a spatula, then invert the pan onto a cutting board and let the cookie come free. Remove the pan and reinvert the cookie onto the wire rack. Cool for 5 minutes more before slicing into wedges to serve.

Brownie Cookies

Servings: 3
Cooking Time: 9 Minutes
Ingredients:
- 2/3 cup shortening
- 1 1/2 cups brown sugar, packed
- 1 tablespoon water

- 1 teaspoon vanilla
- 2 eggs
- 1 1/3 cups flour
- 1/3 cup unsweetened baking cocoa
- 1/4 teaspoon baking soda
- 1/2 teaspoon salt
- 12 ounces semi-sweet chocolate chips

Directions:
1. Preheat the toaster oven to 375°F.
2. With flat beater, cream shortening and brown sugar on medium setting until blended.
3. Add water, vanilla, and eggs and mix. Add flour, cocoa, baking soda, and salt and beat at a medium setting until thoroughly mixed.
4. Stir in chocolate chips on low setting.
5. Drop tablespoons of dough on ungreased baking sheets.
6. Bake 7 to 9 minutes. Do not overcook.

Graham Cracker Crust

Servings: 4
Cooking Time: 14 Minutes
Ingredients:
- 1⅓ cups reduced-fat graham cracker crumbs
- 2 tablespoons brown sugar
- 1 teaspoon ground cinnamon
- Salt to taste
- 1 tablespoon margarine
- 2 tablespoons vegetable oil

Directions:
1. Process the graham crackers in a food processor or blender to produce finely ground crumbs. Add the sugar, cinnamon, and salt and blend by stirring. Set aside.
2. Heat the margarine and oil under a broiler for 4 minutes, or until the margarine is almost melted. Remove from the oven and stir until the margarine is completely melted. Add the graham cracker crumbs and mix thoroughly.
3. Press the mixture into a 9¾-inch pie pan, spreading it out evenly from the middle and up the sides of the pan.
4. BAKE at 350° F. for 10 minutes, or until lightly browned. Cool before filling.

Blueberry Cookies

Servings: 4
Cooking Time: 12 Minutes
Ingredients:
- 1 egg
- 1 tablespoon margarine, at room temperature
- ⅓ cup sugar
- 1¼ cups unbleached flour
- Salt to taste
- 1 teaspoon baking powder
- 1 10-ounce package frozen blueberries, well drained, or
- 1½ cups fresh blueberries, rinsed and drained

Directions:

1. Preheat the toaster oven to 400° F.
2. Beat together the egg, margarine, and sugar in a medium bowl with an electric mixer until smooth. Add the flour, salt, and baking powder, mixing thoroughly. Gently stir in the blueberries just to blend. Do not overmix.
3. Drop by teaspoonfuls on an oiled or nonstick 6½ × 10-inch baking sheet or an oiled or nonstick 8½ × 8½ × 2-inch square baking (cake) pan.
4. BAKE for 12 minutes, or until the cookies are golden brown.

Blackberry Pie

Servings: 6
Cooking Time: 30 Minutes

Ingredients:
• Filling:
• 2 16-ounce bags frozen blackberries, thawed, or 2 cups fresh blackberries, washed and well drained
• 1 4-ounce jar baby food prunes
• 2 tablespoons cornstarch
• 3 ¼ cup brown sugar
• 1 tablespoon lemon juice
• Salt to taste
• 1 Graham Cracker Crust, baked (recipe follows)
• Meringue Topping (recipe follows)

Directions:

1. Preheat the toaster oven to 350° F.
2. Combine the filling ingredients in a large bowl, mixing well. Spoon the filling into the baked Graham Cracker Crust and spread evenly.
3. BAKE for 30 minutes. When cool, top with the Meringue Topping.

Chocolate Cupcakes With Salted Caramel Buttercream

Servings: 12
Cooking Time: 20 Minutes

Ingredients:
• Cake Ingredients
• 1 egg
• ½ cup vegetable oil
• ½ cup buttermilk
• ½ teaspoon vanilla extract
• 1 cup granulated sugar
• 1 cup all-purpose flour
• ¼ cup dark cocoa powder
• 1 teaspoon baking soda
• ½ teaspoon salt
• ½ teaspoon instant espresso powder
• ½ cup boiling water (205°-212°F)
• Buttercream Ingredients
• ½ cup unsalted butter, room temperature

• ⅓ cup caramel sauce, room temperature
• ½ teaspoon vanilla extract
• ½ teaspoon kosher salt
• 1 cup powdered sugar

Directions:

1. Whisk together the egg, vegetable oil, buttermilk, and vanilla extract in a bowl and set aside.
2. Sift together sugar, flour, cocoa powder, baking soda, salt, and instant espresso in a large mixing bowl.
3. Add the wet ingredients into the dry and mix until well combined.
4. Pour in the boiling water slowly while whisking vigorously until the batter is smooth.
5. Line the muffin pan with cupcake liners, then pour in the batter.
6. Preheat the toaster Oven to 350°F.
7. Place the cupcakes on the wire rack, then insert the rack at mid position in the preheated oven.
8. Select the Bake and Fan functions, adjust time to 20 minutes, and press Start/Pause.
9. Remove when done and allow cupcakes to cool on a wire rack for 2 hours.
10. Beat butter using a stand mixer on medium speed for 1 minute or until smooth and fluffy.
11. Beat in the caramel sauce, vanilla, and salt for 2 minutes or until well combined. You may need to scrape down the side of the bowl occasionally.
12. Add the powdered sugar slowly, beating on low speed until fully incorporated.
13. Beat the buttercream on medium speed for 2 minutes or until smooth and creamy.
14. Pipe the buttercream onto the cooled cupcake using a decorated tip.
15. Place the cakes in the fridge for 30 minutes before serving.

Coconut Rice Cake

Servings: 8
Cooking Time: 30 Minutes

Ingredients:
• 1 cup all-natural coconut water
• 1 cup unsweetened coconut milk
• 1 teaspoon almond extract
• ¼ teaspoon salt
• 4 tablespoons honey
• cooking spray
• ¾ cup raw jasmine rice
• 2 cups sliced or cubed fruit

Directions:

1. In a medium bowl, mix together the coconut water, coconut milk, almond extract, salt, and honey.
2. Spray air fryer oven baking pan with cooking spray and add the rice.
3. Pour liquid mixture over rice.

4. Preheat the toaster oven to 360°F and air-fry for 15 minutes. Stir and air-fry for 15 minutes longer or until rice grains are tender.

5. Allow cake to cool slightly. Run a dull knife around edge of cake, inside the pan. Turn the cake out onto a platter and garnish with fruit.

Individual Peach Crisps

Servings: 2
Cooking Time: 60 Minutes
Ingredients:
- 2 tablespoons granulated sugar, divided
- 1 teaspoon lemon juice
- ¼ teaspoon cornstarch
- ⅛ teaspoon table salt, divided
- 1 pound frozen sliced peaches, thawed
- ⅓ cup whole almonds or pecans, chopped fine
- ¼ cup (1¼ ounces) all-purpose flour
- 2 tablespoons packed light brown sugar
- ⅛ teaspoon ground cinnamon
- Pinch ground nutmeg
- 3 tablespoons unsalted butter, melted and cooled

Directions:
1. Adjust toaster oven rack to lowest position and preheat the toaster oven to 425 degrees. Combine 1 tablespoon granulated sugar, lemon juice, cornstarch, and pinch salt in medium bowl. Gently toss peaches with sugar mixture and divide evenly between two 12-ounce ramekins.

2. Combine almonds, flour, brown sugar, cinnamon, nutmeg, remaining pinch salt, and remaining 1 tablespoon granulated sugar in now-empty bowl. Drizzle with melted butter and toss with fork until evenly moistened and mixture forms large chunks with some pea-size pieces throughout. Sprinkle topping evenly over peaches, breaking up any large chunks.

3. Place ramekins on aluminum foil–lined small rimmed baking sheet and bake until filling is bubbling around edges and topping is deep golden brown, 25 to 30 minutes, rotating sheet halfway through baking. Let crisps cool on wire rack for 15 minutes before serving.

Blueberry Crisp

Servings: 6
Cooking Time: 13 Minutes
Ingredients:
- 3 cups Fresh or thawed frozen blueberries
- ⅓ cup Granulated white sugar
- 1 tablespoon Instant tapioca
- ⅓ cup All-purpose flour
- ⅓ cup Rolled oats (not quick-cooking or steel-cut)
- ⅓ cup Chopped walnuts or pecans
- ⅓ cup Packed light brown sugar
- 5 tablespoons plus 1 teaspoon (⅔ stick) Butter, melted

and cooled
- ¾ teaspoon Ground cinnamon
- ¼ teaspoon Table salt

Directions:
1. Preheat the toaster oven to 400°F.

2. Mix the blueberries, granulated white sugar, and instant tapioca in a 6-inch round cake pan for a small batch, a 7-inch round cake pan for a medium batch, or an 8-inch round cake pan for a large batch.

3. When the machine is at temperature, set the cake pan in the air fryer oven and air-fry undisturbed for 5 minutes, or just until the blueberries begin to bubble.

4. Meanwhile, mix the flour, oats, nuts, brown sugar, butter, cinnamon, and salt in a medium bowl until well combined.

5. When the blueberries have begun to bubble, crumble this flour mixture evenly on top. Continue air-frying undisturbed for 8 minutes, or until the topping has browned a bit and the filling is bubbling.

6. Use two hot pads or silicone baking mitts to transfer the cake pan to a wire rack. Cool for at least 10 minutes or to room temperature before serving.

Orange-glazed Brownies

Servings: 12
Cooking Time: 30 Minutes
Ingredients:
- 3 squares unsweetened chocolate
- 3 tablespoons margarine
- 1 cup sugar
- ½ cup orange juice
- 2 eggs
- 1½ cups unbleached flour
- 1 teaspoon baking powder
- Salt to taste
- 1 tablespoon grated orange zest
- Orange Glaze (recipe follows)

Directions:
1. BROIL the chocolate and margarine in an oiled or non-stick 8½ × 8½ × 2-inch square baking (cake) pan for 3 minutes, or until almost melted. Remove from the oven and stir until completely melted. Transfer the chocolate/margarine mixture to a medium bowl.

2. Beat in the sugar, orange juice, and eggs with an electric mixer. Stir in the flour, baking powder, salt, and orange zest and mix until well blended. Pour into the oiled or nonstick square cake pan.

3. BAKE at 350° F. for 30 minutes, or until a toothpick inserted in the center comes out clean. Make holes over the entire top by piercing with a fork or toothpick. Paint with Orange Glaze and cut into squares.

Strawberry Blueberry Cobbler

Servings: 6
Cooking Time: 30 Minutes
Ingredients:
- Berry filling:
- 1 10-ounce package frozen blueberries, thawed, or 1½ cups fresh blueberries
- 1 10-ounce package frozen strawberries, thawed, or 1½ cups fresh strawberries
- ½ cup strawberry preserves
- ¼ cup unbleached flour
- 1 teaspoon lemon juice
- Topping:
- ¼ cup unbleached flour
- 2 tablespoons margarine
- 1 tablespoon fat-free half-and-half
- ½ teaspoon baking powder
- 1 tablespoon sugar

Directions:
1. Preheat the toaster oven to 400° F.
2. Combine the berry filling ingredients in a large bowl, mixing well. Transfer to an oiled or nonstick 8½ × 8½ × 2-inch square baking (cake) pan. Set aside.
3. Combine the topping ingredients in a small bowl, blending with a fork until the mixture is crumbly. Sprinkle the mixture evenly over the berries.
4. BAKE for 30 minutes, or until the top is lightly browned.

Raspberry Hand Pies

Servings: 6
Cooking Time: 20 Minutes
Ingredients:
- 2 cups fresh raspberries
- ¼ cup granulated sugar, plus extra for topping
- 1 tablespoon cornstarch
- 1 tablespoon freshly squeezed lemon juice
- 2 store-bought unbaked pie crusts
- 1 large egg
- 1 tablespoon water
- Oil spray (hand-pumped)

Directions:
1. Preheat the toaster oven to 350°F on AIR FRY for 5 minutes.
2. Place the air-fryer basket in the baking tray.
3. In a medium bowl, stir the raspberries, sugar, cornstarch, and lemon juice until well mixed.
4. Lay the pie crusts on a clean work surface and cut out 6 (6-inch) circles.
5. Evenly divide the raspberry mixture among the circles, placing it in the center.
6. In a small bowl, beat together the egg and water with a fork. Use the egg wash to lightly moisten the edges of the circles, then fold them over to create a half-moon shape. Use a fork to crimp around the rounded part of the pies to seal.
7. Lightly spray the pies with the oil and sprinkle with sugar. Cut 2 to 3 small slits in each pie and place three pies in the basket.
8. In position 2, air fry for 10 minutes until golden brown. Repeat with the remaining pies.
9. Cool the pies and serve.

Sweet Potato Donut Holes

Servings: 18
Cooking Time: 4 Minutes
Ingredients:
- 1 cup flour
- ⅓ cup sugar
- ¼ teaspoon baking soda
- 1 teaspoon baking powder
- ⅛ teaspoon salt
- ½ cup cooked mashed purple sweet potatoes
- 1 egg, beaten
- 2 tablespoons butter, melted
- 1 teaspoon pure vanilla extract
- oil for misting or cooking spray

Directions:
1. Preheat the toaster oven to 390°F.
2. In a large bowl, stir together the flour, sugar, baking soda, baking powder, and salt.
3. In a separate bowl, combine the potatoes, egg, butter, and vanilla and mix well.
4. Add potato mixture to dry ingredients and stir into a soft dough.
5. Shape dough into 1½-inch balls. Mist lightly with oil or cooking spray.
6. Place 9 donut holes in air fryer oven, leaving a little space in between. Air-fry for 4 minutes, until done in center and lightly browned outside.
7. Repeat step 6 to cook remaining donut holes.

Recipe for:

Ingredients:

Equipment:

Description:

Instructions:

Date: _____

MY SHOPPING LIST

Appendix A : Measurement Conversions

BASIC KITCHEN CONVERSIONS & EQUIVALENTS

DRY MEASUREMENTS CONVERSION CHART

3 TEASPOONS = 1 TABLESPOON = 1/16 CUP

6 TEASPOONS = 2 TABLESPOONS = 1/8 CUP

12 TEASPOONS = 4 TABLESPOONS = 1/4 CUP

24 TEASPOONS = 8 TABLESPOONS = 1/2 CUP

36 TEASPOONS = 12 TABLESPOONS = 3/4 CUP

48 TEASPOONS = 16 TABLESPOONS = 1 CUP

METRIC TO US COOKING CONVERSIONS

OVEN TEMPERATURES

120 °C = 250 °F

160 °C = 320 °F

180° C = 350 °F

205 °C = 400 °F

220 °C = 425 °F

LIQUID MEASUREMENTS CONVERSION CHART

8 FLUID OUNCES = 1 CUP = 1/2 PINT = 1/4 QUART

16 FLUID OUNCES = 2 CUPS = 1 PINT = 1/2 QUART

32 FLUID OUNCES = 4 CUPS = 2 PINTS = 1 QUART

= 1/4 GALLON

128 FLUID OUNCES = 16 CUPS = 8 PINTS = 4 QUARTS = 1 GALLON

BAKING IN GRAMS

1 CUP FLOUR = 140 GRAMS

1 CUP SUGAR = 150 GRAMS

1 CUP POWDERED SUGAR = 160 GRAMS

1 CUP HEAVY CREAM = 235 GRAMS

VOLUME

1 MILLILITER = 1/5 TEASPOON

5 ML = 1 TEASPOON

15 ML = 1 TABLESPOON

240 ML = 1 CUP OR 8 FLUID OUNCES

1 LITER = 34 FL. OUNCES

WEIGHT

1 GRAM = .035 OUNCES

100 GRAMS = 3.5 OUNCES

500 GRAMS = 1.1 POUNDS

1 KILOGRAM = 35 OUNCES

US TO METRIC COOKING CONVERSIONS

1/5 TSP = 1 ML

1 TSP = 5 ML

1 TBSP = 15 ML

1 FL OUNCE = 30 ML

1 CUP = 237 ML

1 PINT (2 CUPS) = 473 ML

1 QUART (4 CUPS) = .95 LITER

1 GALLON (16 CUPS) = 3.8 LITERS

1 OZ = 28 GRAMS

1 POUND = 454 GRAMS

BUTTER

1 CUP BUTTER = 2 STICKS = 8 OUNCES = 230 GRAMS = 8 TABLESPOONS

WHAT DOES 1 CUP EQUAL

1 CUP = 8 FLUID OUNCES

1 CUP = 16 TABLESPOONS

1 CUP = 48 TEASPOONS

1 CUP = 1/2 PINT

1 CUP = 1/4 QUART

1 CUP = 1/16 GALLON

1 CUP = 240 ML

BAKING PAN CONVERSIONS

1 CUP ALL-PURPOSE FLOUR = 4.5 OZ

1 CUP ROLLED OATS = 3 OZ 1 LARGE EGG = 1.7 OZ

1 CUP BUTTER = 8 OZ 1 CUP MILK = 8 OZ

1 CUP HEAVY CREAM = 8.4 OZ

1 CUP GRANULATED SUGAR = 7.1 OZ

1 CUP PACKED BROWN SUGAR = 7.75 OZ

1 CUP VEGETABLE OIL = 7.7 OZ

1 CUP UNSIFTED POWDERED SUGAR = 4.4 OZ

BAKING PAN CONVERSIONS

9-INCH ROUND CAKE PAN = 12 CUPS

10-INCH TUBE PAN =16 CUPS

11-INCH BUNDT PAN = 12 CUPS

9-INCH SPRINGFORM PAN = 10 CUPS

9 X 5 INCH LOAF PAN = 8 CUPS

9-INCH SQUARE PAN = 8 CUPS

Appendix B : Recipes Index

Made in the USA
Columbia, SC
12 December 2024